# PRAISE FOR CHRIS RILEY

Chris' kindness is only paralleled by his accuracy and guidance. He cuts through so quickly and sharply with the kind of information even those closest to me haven't known. He has a true gift of sight, and I am lucky enough to have experienced it.

*Kat Graham, actress,* The Vampire Diaries

A treasure trove of knowledge that must be read by those interested in awakening their psychic potential. This is your opportunity to be guided by a world-class psychic, Chris Riley.

*Claire Stone, spiritual author and award-winning psychic development expert*

I had a reading done by Chris and it was the most incredible experience I could ever have hoped for. He knew things nobody would have known, helped me have a clearer vision on my life's direction and left me feeling so comforted by connecting with my loved ones. I'm very grateful to Chris and I can't recommend him enough. Chris, you are amazing.

*Siannise Fudge,* Love Island UK, *Season 6*

Chris, who is a real-deal psychic super-talent – I bloody love him! – has generously shared all of his wisdom, skills and expertise (and secrets) to help you to unlock *your* psychic powers. If you want to know how to connect with your Higher Self, what it means when you see 11.11, how to access your extra-sensory gifts or what crystal to use to attract luck, Chris, in his honest and relatable style, has written this book for *you*!

*Lisa Lister, author of* Witch, Presence,
Code Red and Self Source-ery

Chris' insight into the psychic world feels unique, fresh, genuine, comforting and full of hope.

*Naomi Channell, TV producer and host
of true-crime podcast* Real

# You
# MUST BE
# PSYCHIC

# *You* MUST BE PSYCHIC

## Secrets to unlock your inner power and reveal your future

### CHRIS RILEY

HarperCollins*Publishers*

Thorsons
An imprint of HarperCollins*Publishers*
1 London Bridge Street
London SE1 9GF
www.harpercollins.co.uk

HarperCollins*Publishers*
Macken House, 39/40 Mayor Street Upper
Dublin 1, D01 C9W8, Ireland

First published by Thorsons 2024

3 5 7 9 10 8 6 4 2

# CONTENTS

# INTRODUCTION

I grew up in a very rural area, a quiet one, a village that not many people know of on the outskirts of Essex towards Suffolk. I went to a quiet primary school as well; I was one of only around twenty children there.

I was often quite an anxious and nervous child. I kept myself to myself through my younger years and I always found it hard to trust and open up to people. The anxiety and the nervousness would often come from the thoughts and feelings I couldn't understand. I would look at people and think things that I knew were not my own thoughts. Or I'd have thoughts that you wouldn't normally have, for instance, looking at someone and thinking, 'She's just had an argument with her partner.'

I remember one particular time I was at school, looking at my teacher and thinking that she would have a baby, and it was just a few weeks later that she came into class and announced her pregnancy.

Neither I nor anyone else could explain how I knew the things I knew, so I'd often dismiss what I thought. My family didn't really trust what I said, and I think it frightened them, so they would often just ignore it. I was never encouraged; instead, I was told I was strange or different. If only I'd known then this was a psychic ability, a real gift, and trusted it in the way that I do now.

As I'm writing this, I'm 28 years old, but I want to take you back to one of my very earliest memories. I was just 8 years old when I had my first psychic experience, that I can remember anyhow. I went to bed one night and I had the strange feeling that someone was going to break into our home. I just couldn't shake the feeling. It was horrible.

I couldn't sleep. I crept quietly to the front door, and it was only partially locked. So, I dropped the latch and engaged a second lock, and off to bed I went. At around 2 a.m. I was awoken by loud banging. It sounded as if someone was thumping on the door, but in fact they were trying to kick it in.

It was a huge relief for the family that I had locked the door, as it stopped the supposed burglar from getting in. But my predictions didn't stop there. I felt that the person who had done this wasn't far away, and I said this repeatedly for weeks on end.

Four years on, we found out that it was in fact our neighbour who had done this. He'd been at the pub at the end of the road, hence not far away, and we assumed that he'd returned home intoxicated and mistaken our house for his own, and the fact that he was unable to get in had led to him getting frustrated and attempting to kick the door in.

It took me years before I truly realized that the thoughts and feelings I was having weren't just thoughts, but were intuitive feelings.

I believe that we all have intuitive feelings and psychic ability within us, but for some of us it is naturally more evident. We become aware of it through the experiences we have, whereas for others it may be a little harder to connect with.

I have often found that the psychic senses can be triggered by trauma. In my own life I've found that the more loss and trauma I experience, the more my psychic ability has both strengthened and sharpened. Certain experiences I have had in my life have definitely caused me to be more empathetic, more understanding and more compassionate, too, allowing me to guide others and work as a psychic medium.

I hope that this book will be helpful to you in understanding the psychic world and understanding your own experiences. I hope it will allow you to connect with your own psychic gift and with the spirit world.

I have always believed in taking what feels right to me and leaving what doesn't behind, and I recommend this approach to you as you read on.

To help you on your way, I will include plenty of affirmations, exercises and other things you can do. Affirmations are a powerful way of clearing your mind of limiting self-beliefs, negative thoughts and anything else that may be holding you back both in life and as you develop your psychic abilities. Here's an example:

> **Affirmation:** 'I know that the trauma in my life has led me to be kinder and more caring. I can use the experiences I've had to help and guide others.'

One important thing to be reminded of is that each and every one of us is learning and growing every day. I find that I am always discovering new things about my gift and expanding my knowledge.

Everything that I share within this book is truly from my heart, and I hope you find it useful and insightful.

*Chris Riley*

# 1

# PSYCHIC ABILITY AND THE EMPATH NATURE

I have always said that being psychic is a blessing and a curse. When people find out I'm psychic, they are either in awe or want me to instantly give them a reading or some sort of proof that it is real. They also tend to tell me how lucky I am. Yes, I do feel very blessed, and I never expected my life to progress in the way that it has. Yet I do believe in destiny and I do believe in fate, therefore I know that I am doing this for a reason.

I never chose to be psychic, but I like to say I was chosen to be. Just as someone can have a talent for acting or music, I have this talent, or 'gift', as some like to call it.

It took me some years to realize I was psychic, but now I have learned to embrace it. I wouldn't trade it for anything. I get to meet the most incredible people from all walks of life, I get to witness my clients having the most amazing transformations, and I get to guide them along the way, to help them better themselves and be the best they can be. Ultimately, that's the goal of any psychic: to help, to guide and to empower.

I'm very blessed and honoured to have this gift. But what exactly is it?

# Psychic Ability

You may have heard people say they are psychic or a medium, as these are the terms commonly used to define this ability that some of us have. Sometimes 'psychic', 'intuitive' and 'medium' are considered to be one and the same, but this is not the case. Just as a small cheat sheet:

*Psychic*: Psychic ability is the ability to sense, feel or know things about other people. It can also bring you visions of the future.

*Intuitive*: To be intuitive is to have a clear connection to your own gut feelings and inner guidance.

*Medium*: Mediumship is the ability to connect with loved ones who have passed away and convey precise, specific details about them with the intention of bringing proof of eternal life and bringing healing and closure to someone after the loss of a loved one.

So, a psychic is someone who has the ability to sense things about someone's earthbound life to help and guide them. Psychics normally share their insights with those seeking guidance on matters such as love, career or past, present and future. Often, being psychic also requires the skills of a counsellor or therapist. You need to be compassionate, understanding and patient with a client, as often personal matters are discussed and emotions come to the surface in a reading.

Psychic senses normally become evident at a young age, due to our minds usually being clearer then, and this makes us more susceptible to picking up information and feelings from others and our environment. As we reach teenage years and adulthood, most of us find it harder to connect with our psychic senses, as our minds are often clouded or preoccupied with our busy lives. In childhood, we are in a 'purer' state; we've often arrived (incarnated) with a full set of memories and wisdom intact from other lives. Our consciousness is pure, clean and energized. So, when we are kids, we see through a clearer lens – we possess vision coupled with clear sight and instincts.

Many of us who are psychic receive information through feelings, voices or thoughts. You may have noticed you have thought and felt things that seemed strange or out of the ordinary. For example, you may have looked at someone and seen them smiling, but just known that wasn't genuine. Or perhaps you just knew you couldn't trust someone, despite what they said, and that person quickly broke your trust. Situations like these are very common signs of being in tune with psychic ability and intuition, and perhaps you are naturally in touch with your own psychic senses.

Yet many people who are psychic find their ability has been almost buried by trauma, hurt and pain. Through my journey as a psychic, I have often connected with other psychics who have experienced severe pain and trauma in their younger life. Those painful moments in our younger years allow us to handle emotional situations with more compassion and empathy, but we are naturally conditioned to avoid pain, and many of us will shut away something that causes us to feel any more hurt or pain.

Unfortunately, psychic ability isn't something that many people understand, so often people are afraid of it or don't trust it, and tell those with psychic ability not to delve into it.

On that note, I don't strictly follow protection rituals or practices, but I do recommend that whatever your faith and beliefs, you invite protection from that source, if you feel the need or feel more comfortable doing that. (*For more on protection, see page 112.*)

Sometimes we shut ourselves off from something to protect ourselves, and perhaps you have shut your psychic ability off or put it to one side because of what someone else made you think or believe. If you feel that in the past you had more psychic experiences than you currently do and you would like to regain your psychic senses, then there are some ways which I would love to share with you that may help you in reopening those senses and helping them to become more apparent and available to you in your day-to-day life.

# The Empath Nature

Psychic abilities go hand in hand with being an empath. This means you take 'being empathic' a step further and naturally feel what others feel. And feel it very deeply – it's as though you're soaking up someone's emotions in their entirety, good or bad, and making them your own. This can be extremely exhausting mentally.

It may also mean it's difficult to have close contact with others, and finding yourself in crowded or busy places may be challenging. I've definitely struggled with the latter, purely because I'm so sensitive to the feelings of others. Sometimes everything can feel magnified, everything can feel a lot heavier, and sounds can feel a lot louder than they really are. I feel very sensitive when in busy crowds or noisy environments. When you are an empath, you may definitely feel aggravated by chaotic surroundings.

The important thing is to be gentle with yourself and always remember you are only human and you are doing your best.

At such moments, be as caring towards yourself as you are towards others. People who describe themselves as empaths are normally very caring, nurturing and gentle. It's in their nature. They always want to make sure that other people have the things they need to feel happy, safe and loved.

Are you someone who takes care of others before yourself? Do you feel more selfless than selfish or self-serving? Are you a giver with a heart of gold who puts the needs of children, animals, nature and other people before your own? If so, you might be destined for the path of the healer, psychic or medium!

I'd like to run through the key qualities of an empath, as these are definite clues to the presence of innate psychic abilities, either currently accessed or not yet harnessed. Then we'll go on to look at the main ways in which these qualities manifest.

## Key qualities

### Telepathic abilities
Empaths can read minds, either literally or through advanced instinctive, empathic and emotionally intelligent capabilities. They possess telepathic abilities similar to those of dolphins, who can 'hear' through supersonic sound waves.

### Extra-sensory gifts
Like snakes and other creatures (elephants, bats, dogs), empaths can sense vibrations and energy through the Ether. They feel, sense, see, hear and know, intuitively, in

a way that many people don't. They sense distortions and imbalances in others' energy fields; they possess a special superhuman radar that cannot be explained rationally or logically. They are connected to the unseen realms and dimensions around us.

## Emotional intelligence

Emotional intelligence is well developed in empaths. They navigate life with a strong need for emotional bonds and connection, as well as the ability to help others through their advanced emotional frequency. Empaths feel things so deeply that boundaries are normally crossed. Positively, this allows them to be amazing healers, visionaries and so forth.

## Master intuitives

Empaths are master intuitives with the ability to pick up on subtle and even hidden thoughts, feelings, emotions and beliefs. A person's – or animal's – whole identity, including their character, strengths, weaknesses, fears and past history, can be felt and seen by an empath. Empathy is, in essence, the ability to feel what it's like to be in another person's shoes (or paws!), and in empaths, this ability is highly developed.

## Selflessness and helpfulness

Empaths are incredibly selfless and helpful. They're service-oriented beings who are able to tune into others' difficulties, doubts, physical ailments and emotional, spiritual and psychological problems. Remember that empaths serve from the heart and, more often than not, the soul, rather than from the ego.

## Choosing a healing, counselling or charitable path

Nearly all empaths choose to become healers, counsellors, therapists, nurses, vets, physicians, spiritual teachers, Tarot readers, psychics, astrologers, humanitarians, aid or charity workers, environmentalists or mediums. Healing is a core part of their DNA and their life purpose.

## Creating peace and harmony

Empaths hate disharmony, injustice and violence. Cruelty, coldness and violence of any kind can even send them into depression, isolation or apathy. To thrive, they need emotionally serene, kind, gentle-hearted, good-natured and supportive people around them.

# Embodied empaths

As an empath, you can embody any one or a mix of the following! I have found myself familiar with all of these on my own journey as a psychic and medium.

## The caregiver/nurturer

All empaths are natural caregivers and counsellors. They have such a strong desire to nurture others that they usually choose a career in the caring professions, as a care or support worker, or nurse, for example. In their spare time, they may volunteer with a homeless shelter or animal sanctuary. Whatever they do, they embody evolved feminine instincts.

If you're familiar with astrology, you'll see that the empath is the ultimate 'Cancer person'. The only zodiac sign ruled by the Moon herself, with the Moon representing emotions, feelings, instincts, feminine wisdom, intuition, sacred knowledge and ancestral wisdom, Cancer is known as the empath of the zodiac. Everything related to the unseen and both subconscious and spiritual worlds also comes under Cancer's influence. It's very handy to be aware of this and you may wish to read up on the Cancer Sun sign to understand your empathic nature better and check out where Cancer's influence falls in your birth chart.

While on the subject of astrology, empathy is usually possessed by Water and Earth Sun signs or people with a lot of Water or Earth in their charts.

## Signs and their elements

*Air signs:* Gemini, Libra and Aquarius
*Water signs:* Cancer, Scorpio and Pisces
*Earth signs:* Taurus, Virgo and Capricorn
*Fire signs:* Aries, Leo and Sagittarius

Another key piece of wisdom here comes from numerology. Empaths are master intuitives, which is symbolic of life path 11, so learning more about life path 11 can help you grow, prosper and attune to innate psychic gifts too, whether this is your own life path or not. If you want to find out your own personal life path number, there are many online resources that you may refer to.

You may also find it interesting to consider the famous '11:11' number sequence, something that a lot of us start to see when we begin to awaken to our spiritual gifts. (*More on 11:11 on page 84.*)

## The BS detector

All empaths are BS detectors, because as an empath, you are an emotional sponge, whether you like it or not. You sense things others can't and look below the surface. So, you can see through the veil of illusion in a way that enables you to see deception, manipulation and false intentions. This can help you individually on a personal level and collectively on a planetary level. It helps you in intimate relationships, business bonds, family ties and everyday relating, including in the service you provide to others. Also, if you wish to become a creative visionary, for instance, or artist of any type, you can use this gift to uncover and depict universal truths.

Truth is actually a keyword for empaths. The ability to connect with others on an advanced emotional, spiritual and psychological frequency opens doorways to higher truth. You are a guiding light to others, or can be.

Being so open and receptive to wisdom and spiritual energies also enhances your self-knowledge, as well as multi-dimensional perception. Not only can you help others through being a guide through toxicity, trauma, shadow setbacks and faulty or distorted belief systems and mind-sets, but you can understand and heal yourself in the process.

Honed empathic gifts provide the basis for all other mediumship and healing skills, which then activate ancient wisdom and memory about your core nature. This can include soul memory for self-alignment, abundance and letting go of old cycles and thought patterns, so you can step into your true role and purpose on this Earth plane, whatever it may be.

When you heal others, you heal yourself; when you heal yourself through choosing to activate others' talents or gifts, you help them rise to and live in their own truth.

Empathy is a beautiful gift, even though those of us who are psychic or empathic are often seen as weird!

Note, however, that seeing through other people's and society's BS and manipulations does require a strong level of personal strength. Boundaries are key here, and I hope the knowledge I will share in this book will help you develop yours, to make sure you keep your energy and aura protected at all times.

## The intellectual empath

Being an intellectual empath means having the ability to connect or tune into memories and past experiences to help others, for instance merging with another person's or even group's mind and energy field to come up with extraordinary ideas. Amazing authors, writers, poets, speakers, spoken word artists, lecturers, publishers, teachers and researchers possess the gift of intellectual empathy. World-class experts in these fields go on to lead and inspire simply by being courageous enough to move through their own emotional barriers, and as I know myself, that can be tough! Empaths are sponges, as I mentioned earlier, and that is how I have felt most of my life, so I know that through deep and genuine connection with others you can absorb the power of the collective energies, and you will find that other people's energies, thoughts and intentions can affect you deeply.

It takes some strength, so many empaths tend to turn away from their intellectual side due to weak boundaries.

To go back to astrology for a moment, the Air element is all about communication, speaking, writing, being direct and assertive, speaking up and embodying boldness. Intellectual empaths can read something once and store it on a subconscious or unconscious level. When they need it, they then 'pull' it out of the Ether for inspirational words and works of art.

As an intellectual empath, when you interact with someone, some subtle energy may trigger you into knowing about some seriously complex topics! When you're communicating with others, you can also change your vocabulary, speech and style to the point where you may change roles or personas and start speaking of unusual or specialist subjects. You can essentially adapt to any character, language or culture. It's a miraculous ability to have.

Mirroring behaviour or knowledge can make you into a genius, but it's your own wisdom, on some level, as it's coming from deep within. You may start to ask yourself, 'How do I know this?'

## Parroting tip!

If you want to develop this gift, start to work with the Parrot spirit animal. Parrots are famous for mimicking language and speech. You may then feel more comfortable being around types of people you may not currently mix with.

## The animal communicator

Empaths' ability to empathize doesn't stop at humans – they often have a strong emotional pull to animals too. Animals require only love and care, and in return they bring us only unconditional love. Those of us who are empaths really feel the love that our pets bring to us and may feel a strong emotional connection with them, perhaps more so than with some of the humans in our lives.

Personally, I have always felt a huge connection with animals. I have five beautiful cats and two dogs and two rabbits, and I feel that they were brought to me for a reason. I feel animal communication comes naturally to those of us who are in touch with our intuition. It's not a special gift of the chosen few, it's an ability that we are all born with.

Many of you will have experienced a form of communication with your animal friends or pets without even realizing it. Do you ever just know that your cat or dog isn't feeling well, or is restless, or wants something, just by looking at them? Obviously they can't speak, but they are sending messages to you constantly, which you should sense through your natural intuitiveness. As an empath, you will be able to communicate with all sorts of animal species through eye contact, body language and projected thoughts and emotions. Your sensitivity and gentleness will definitely go out into the space surrounding you. Animals will then pick up on these and feel safe around you and drawn to you.

Feeling the emotions of animals and sensing their past pain, trauma or joy are all common experiences for empaths. Many feel more comfortable around animals than people, as they are non-judgemental. They live in harmony with nature, therefore they are unconditionally loving and compassionate. Moreover, they sense your empathy and respond to it.

Animals are so very clever and time spent with them can be magical.

Animal communicators live from the heart and soul, which diminishes a timeline of fear and aligns them with universal love instead, which unites them with the animal. (*More on timelines later.*)

On a deeper level, we can see how love creates and serves as an unspoken bond – a soul contract taking place on an invisible and soulful or spiritual level. I have always felt that my animals have brought a sensation of calm and peace into my life, and this has definitely helped me when tapping into my own psychic abilities.

## The helper and healer

All empaths are helpers and healers – selfless beings committed to a path of service. Yes, even those of us who go on to make a living through our gifts and enjoy financial prosperity are selfless! Many people believe that having money shows you are greedy, but this is not at all the case. Many psychics, including myself, find it hard to accept money or gifts, and just want to give. However, we need to remember we cannot pour from a glass that's half-full! At the end of the day, we all need money to survive. Think of it as 'root chakra living'. (*More on the chakras later, too.*)

Essentially, as empaths, our primary motivation is to help. We are evolved beings, and this statement isn't coming from a space of arrogance or false hope, but from the knowledge that we give and serve from the heart and higher mind or Higher Self. The Higher Self is a source of divine contact and spiritual power.

One thing I wish to share in alignment with this topic is that empaths never use their psychic gifts for personal gain, whether in the form of status, fame, fortune or admiration and praise. This is never the case, and I want to make this clear: we do what we do from the heart, and we expect nothing other than a heartfelt response in return.

Following on from this, for an empath, no soul is left unnoticed and no one is seen as lesser or better than others, although a grown and self-mastered empath does acknowledge that we all have different talents and that we're all at different stages of our evolutionary journey. It's important to remember that no two people are the same and we each have our own challenges, things we have to deal with or work through, and none of us should be judging another person.

It's the empath's destiny to heal others, whoever they are, either through their wisdom, compassion and presence, which ripple out to affect everyone they meet, or through material acts of service. So, you may have noticed that you have naturally healing hands and a healing presence. People may gravitate towards you; strangers may come up to you and speak about intimate and personal problems. Animals and children feel comfortable around you, as if you're family. You're there for them.

> Did you know that many empaths are powerful healers, shamans, seers, clairvoyants, telepaths, astrologers, mediums and holistic therapists?

## The telepath

This archetypal empath is also known as the medical empath, and it describes those who use their empathic, sensitive and psychic gifts to help others get to the root of their physical ailments. If you are one of these empaths, you may sense when someone has a stomach bug, for instance, or toothache or a strained muscle. They won't give any external cues or clues, you'll just sense it; in fact, your psychic senses will draw you straight to the affected area or body part.

Sometimes, you will even take on the pain for a moment. If you're close to someone and they have a severe migraine, for instance, you'll feel it as if it's your own. You'll share their pain to lessen their burden.

It's magical, awe-inspiring and slightly self-detrimental all in one, and this is why, once again, boundaries are so important.

Many medical empaths go on to become healers or therapists due to this special gift. Some can even see energy blockages directly – a combination of colour and a feeling of internal distortion or imbalance. I have always been able to. I would describe it as body scanning. Through your mind's eye, you can sense and almost visualize health issues or concerns.

## The activist empath

Finally, activist empaths are warrior empaths, the ones who embody great inner strength in order to bring change to the world. They're activists, change-makers, peacekeepers, justice and truth speakers. They stand up and have a voice. They can be scientists, inventors, artists, musicians, speakers, writers, poets, technology experts, teachers of any field, or even politicians. Whatever they do, they believe in justice and truth and stand up for human and animal rights. They may work alone behind the scenes, creating a masterpiece like a book, song or work of art, or as part of a group or team, or stand strong in the spotlight. They make compassionate, fearless and powerful leaders.

Are you someone who is greatly affected by fundraising and charity adverts, or seeing someone who is less fortunate than you are? Are you horrified by the violence, hatred, envy, separation, greed, coldness and injustice of the world? Do you want to do something about that? You may become an activist empath.

Remember, though, that 'boundaries' is a keyword for all empaths. Without boundaries, sometimes people can just dump their problems on us and that can be way too much to handle, resulting in a number of emotional, psychological, physical and spiritual health problems. Empaths may also be vulnerable to manipulation and toxic behaviour. This brings us to the particular struggles we face...

## Empath struggles: Be aware and stay aligned!

It's really beneficial to be in the know about the main empath struggles. You may know about some of them already! In your younger life, you may have been deeply sensitive and compassionate towards all sentient creatures, but as you gained more wisdom from age and life experience, you may have realized you needed boundaries in place. Why? Because empaths can become everyone's doormat. You may already have found that strangers will walk up to you and offload their problems, while friends, family and acquaintances will see you as an easy target, someone to use or mistreat. Also, every healer, empath and psychic comes across unsavoury characters, some more toxic than others. These are sent to us to test us, so we can evolve and transcend our own toxic traits to become the masterful intuitives we were born to be.

As you open yourself up as a channel to heal and help others with your unique gifts, you will undoubtedly start to attract toxic people. These people are there to help you grow, but sometimes that in itself can be, as I have found, the hardest pill to swallow.

What sort of people are they? The first is the narcissist, or person with narcissistic personality disorder.

## Dealing with narcissists

This is one of the most brutal tests you can face. Narcissists are vicious, venomous and completely destructive to your spirit, inner strength and empathic gifts. While you are a giver, they are takers. While you embody kindness, grace and gentleness, they are mean-spirited users. They seek to take all of your light, beauty, kindness, self-esteem, self-love and capacity for creating abundance and sincere connections.

I'm sure you have met at least one of these people in your life or know one. They aren't easily forgotten. Narcissists are extremely manipulative, selfish and self-serving people who can gaslight you, which is distorting the truth to make you believe you are crazy. They completely dismiss real words, events and actions, and make you believe you're delusional and that your kindness, humility, integrity, grace and nobility aren't real. In truth, *they* are the liars. They deceive, cheat and con others, and they get a kick out of doing so, as it boosts their ego. They twist and distort truth and reality, and then make you out to be something you're not. Narcissists are completely self-serving, self-entitled and self-righteous people who wear a mask. They appear charming, bright and kind in a social setting, but behind closed doors they are the total opposite. They're massive con artists who steal your light and inner beauty and use it for their own personal gain.

All empaths attract narcissists. You're their personal source of power. Unfortunately, they see compassion, empathy and kindness as weaknesses, and consider sweetness and nurturing opportunities for abuse. They are verbally, emotionally and psychologically abusive, and use gaslighting as a major tactic to keep the illusion of control. That's all it is – an illusion. The secret to breaking free is knowing it's an illusion. You are not bound to them and they have no control over you.

## My advice for dealing with narcissists:

1. Avoid them! You don't need this abuse in your life.

2. If you unconsciously enter into a relationship with a narcissist, remember that it is the ultimate test, the final chapter, if you will, before your true life begins. A relationship with a narcissist is a catalyst to embracing your true path and purpose as a healer or psychic.

3. Develop boundaries and take self-protection measures. Doing so is paramount to healing and reclaiming your sovereignty, which will in turn lead to psychic self-development and mastery.

## Dealing with energy vampires and other toxic personalities

### Energy vampires

Energy vampires are common too, as, like narcissists, they are very attracted to the light of empaths and seek to take it.

Energy vampires make you feel guilty for shining, showing your soul and being empathic. Their identity is rooted in what they can take and gain, and that is what they are focused on, not what they can give or how they can serve. Toxic characters such as these intentionally try to keep you down and keep negative or unhealthy karmic cycles and patterns on repeat. There's little sincerity to them. You'll know you're dealing with one because they'll make you feel guilty when luck or abundance or happiness comes into your life.

Tied in here is the personality distortion I like to call 'the jealous one'. Jealous ones take envy and jealousy a step further than negative feelings. Severely jealous people can make it their life's mission to destroy you, simply because they are jealous of your gifts and self-worth, and possible fame or success. Extremely jealous people try to convince you that your energy is not your own. If they can't have it, why should you?

There are some genuinely cold-hearted and mean-spirited people in this world. Some people can't be happy for anyone to be genuine, spiritual and enlightened, to whatever degree, and this has definitely been one of my hardest lessons to learn.

But remember, nothing should come between you and your life's mission, and people like this carry deep pain, trauma and self-loathing within. They aren't happy with themselves, so how can you expect them to be happy for you?

It's a sad truth, but it's something every empath and healer or psychic or medium will have to come to terms with. The spirit of jealousy is real, so develop your boundaries, work with special healing crystals and put self-protection measures in place. (*For more on protection, see page 112.*)

27

For now, here's a healthy reminder: the spirit of jealousy is one of envy, hate and separation. Jealous people may be excellent actors, yet their core frequency is one rooted in ego and hatred, not heart and soul.

### Cynics and naysayers

The toxic personalities I dislike the most after narcissists and energy vampires are cynics and naysayers. Quite simply, these people will seek to take your light and leave you in darkness, as they haven't found the light yet. They don't believe, and not only do they not believe, but they want to take away your faith too. No matter how much you achieve, how much you shine, or how clear your gifts are, they refuse to accept the truth. You could, quite literally, be standing in front of them actually demonstrating your gifts, and they would not accept them. Cynics and naysayers lack vision and sight. Nothing is real to the cynic. Resentment and jealousy are very strong parts of their make-up, as is judgement. You simply must be a terrible and insincere person, in their eyes.

### Abusers and persecutors

Abusers and persecutors take pleasure in causing others pain, which is difficult for even a normal person to handle. But for a sensitive, compassionate and caring person, it is particularly hurtful. As an empath, you simply don't have the ability to treat others in disgraceful ways. Being cold, calculated and unkind is not in your nature; furthermore, it's something you're strongly opposed to. Cruelty of any kind repels you on a soul level, and these toxic personalities act out fantasies of violence on an emotional and psychological level, if not a physical one.

Spiritual warfare, including psychic attack, is common here, as it is with narcissists. Psychic attack is someone sending you such harmful thoughts that they interfere with your energy field, and therefore your spiritual vibration, and your energy is depleted. You can become depressed, unmotivated, fearful of social interactions and of sharing your gifts.

In this respect, empaths can be likened to the 'witches' burned alive in past centuries. These were, in fact, healers, herbalists, medicine men and, most frequently, intuitive women – women who embodied the divine feminine, with all its wonderful gifts and powers. Christ was hung on the cross for similar crimes, specifically being enlightened and embodying the divine.

Sadly, persecution is something all genuine spiritual people will have to face at some point in their lives. One could even say we have a soul contract with such people. This means we encounter or enter into a relationship with them to evolve and learn important life lessons. Some of the hardest lessons we have to learn can appear when we start on our path of psychic or spiritual development.

It's not an easy path and often it does feel like both a blessing and a curse, but I feel blessed to have the gifts that

I do and to be able to connect with others and bring them guidance and healing. I know it's my purpose.

It helps to remember that the desire to cause us harm is deep and often unconscious in these people. It may arise from deeply ingrained conditioning. They are very much in their ego and really need the help of a loving and supportive empath, but this doesn't mean you should give it to them! It usually takes really deep and soulful displays of genuine compassion to do this, and boundaries are key. You wish to give, but persecutors wish to take, so appeasing them isn't in your best interests. For healing, there needs to be a healthy and balanced flow of energy.

### Compulsive or pathological liars

Compulsive or pathological liars are particularly dangerous to empaths, because of how they will try to take advantage of our weak boundaries and gaslight us. Such extreme and intentional truth-distorting affects us on such a deep level that it can be soul-shattering. Being genuine is one of our greatest strengths, so to be lied to or manipulated on repeat can send us into temporary insanity. Being in a liar's energy field regularly is unhealthy for anyone who is sensitive.

## Toxic traits to transcend

As an empath, you will not only have to deal with the toxic people you are presented with, but also your own toxic traits.

We all have them at some point in our lives, especially when we're younger. Recognizing them is key to recognizing your own innate powers, as well as to taking steps to self-alignment and full-power living. What are they? Typically:

- People-pleasing, appeasing others and lacking boundaries; being everyone's emotional dumping-ground; a real inability to say 'no' – saying 'yes' to the point of depletion and burnout.
- Social anxiety, fear of people, places and large crowds; super-sensitivity and hyper-emotionalism, including excessive crying, worrying, pessimistic thinking and self-doubt.
- Absorbing the pain and feelings of everyone else to the point of letting your own self-care slide.
- Co-dependency – becoming reliant on others, getting lost in the realm of fantasy, addiction, isolation and low mental and emotional health.
- Loneliness, low self-esteem, feeling cut off from the world; depression, lethargy, laziness; a lack of life-force and passion (as a result of taking on everyone else's problems and emotions).

I hope these words have awakened hidden wisdom as well as self-knowledge with regard to your psychic and empathic powers! Now we'll go on to look at another core part of you, one that will be vital in your psychic development.

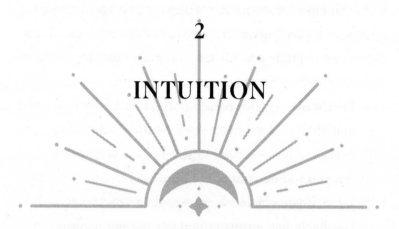

# 2

# INTUITION

Have you ever had an uneasy feeling about something or someone? Have you ever met someone and either had a warm feeling or a horrible feeling in your gut? Or perhaps you've gone to sign a contract for a new home or new job, and out of nowhere it just doesn't feel right? This is your intuition speaking to you and you've probably not even realized.

Intuition is a powerful gift every human on Planet Earth has, but in some people it is more developed than others.

## Being Intuitive vs Being an Intuitive

### Being intuitive

We all have intuitive ability and our intuition is always freely available to us. You are probably using your intuition a whole lot more than you realize.

Your intuition can send you signs in a myriad of ways. Butterflies in your stomach, randomly getting sweaty palms, an image or a feeling can all be manifestations of your intuition trying to guide you. Other potential examples would be suddenly feeling overwhelmed by a generally calm sensation. For me, it's usually a calm inner voice, like a whisper in my mind or heart. I would describe it as my soul guiding me through life.

When you follow your intuition, you'll feel peaceful and happy, but if you choose to go against it or ignore it, then you'll probably feel a wave of anxiety and uneasiness come over you. If you choose to listen to your ego instead of listening to what your heart is trying to tell you, then not only will it not feel right but sooner rather than later you'll know you've messed up. An easy example of this would be giving someone a second chance when they've already hurt you – in your heart you will know that the same thing is likely to happen, but your ego may lead you astray.

## Connecting with your intuition

I have always seen intuition as a muscle: it is always there, but sometimes we need to work it a bit! You'll notice it's easier to connect with your intuition when your mind is clear and as free of stress as possible, but if you're going through a particularly stressful time in your life, you'll tend to find that it's harder to connect with your intuition, and your mind may feel a little clouded. Here's a tip: connecting with your intuition in situations that are stressful can be as simple as placing your hand over your heart when making a decision and asking yourself what is the right thing to do.

If I'm facing a difficult relationship or tough work situation, feeling overwhelmed or have decisions to make, I've actually found my intuition to be louder than usual, and it can often seem more awake.

If you're pushing your intuition away too often or going against it, though, you'll also find it a lot harder to connect with, and not only that, when you do connect with it, you'll find it's harder to trust it.

Talking of trust, as I said earlier, I have always believed in taking on what feels right to me and leaving what doesn't behind. One important thing to be reminded of is that each and every one of us is learning and growing every day. I find that I am always discovering new things about my gift and expanding my knowledge, and my intuition is guiding me along the way.

When you are overly busy, it can be harder to be sensitive to your intuition, so taking time away from your daily life stresses can be a great and easy way to try and be more in tune with it. Spending time in nature is a great way to disconnect from technology and focus on bringing peace and calm into your day. Being mindful of the beauty of the world can help clear out negative, intrusive and distracting thoughts and allow you to focus on the good. A quick intuition boost could be spending five minutes every morning focusing on the good in your life, whether that's people who are there for you, events you can look forward to or everyday things you're grateful for. You can also begin a journal, if you don't already have one, as this is a great way to contemplate and reflect, explore your deepest yearnings and monitor your progress as you develop your talents.

## Being an intuitive

Everyone is intuitive, but being an intuitive is a whole other story. Here are some unique but real signs to look out for:

- ☐ Check out your life path number! If it's 11, you're known as a master intuitive. You can search online to find your life path number.
- ☐ Astrologically, are you one of the three Water signs, Pisces, Cancer and Scorpio? These are the most intuitive signs of all, but your Sun sign isn't everything. You may have a Water Moon or Rising/Ascendant sign, which contributes to being extremely intuitive. I strongly advise researching your birth chart to find out how you operate on a deep and intrinsic level.
- ☐ You can also ask your parents and grandparents if intuitive or psychic gifts run in the family. The chances are you have at least one parent or grandparent who was incredibly intuitive. They may have had herbal

remedies and potions around the house, or even had mediumistic abilities. There's a unique ancestral energy associated with our grandparents, and it's often passed down to younger generations.

# Enhancing your Intuition

When it comes to enhancing your intuition, I highly recommend making meditation a daily practice, as this will help with hearing your intuitive thoughts more clearly.

Here are some exercises that will help you connect more with your intuition in your daily life. Some of these may work better for you than others, so go with your heart and what you feel drawn to practising.

## Creating a *chi* or energy ball

*Chi*, also known as *ki* and *prana*, is the universal life-force energy that flows through all living things. It exists in all the elements – Earth, Water, Fire, Air and Ether or Spirit. A *chi* ball is a 'ball' of *chi*, created through the power of your hands and loving intentions. It is something you can make any time or place with the right intention, for instance during a meditation to activate psychic gifts or when you're out and about and would like to be more in tune with your intuitive thoughts. It's really easy! Yet very effective. A *chi* ball can help heal and move trapped or blocked energy to stimulate important attributes. It can move psychic and intuitive energy up to your third eye and crown chakras and is therefore an excellent technique to master. It's a simple practice, often taught in Reiki and similar healing modalities, but the benefits are remarkable.

For example, creating a *chi* ball for your third eye chakra will stimulate vision, intuition, subtle perception, psychic powers and spiritual abilities, as well as peace of mind, calmness, clarity, peace, higher perspectives and tranquillity. It eases stress, tension and mental distortion, helping to release clouded judgements or muddied perception. It's a great defence against psychic attack and other people's negativities too.

A *chi* ball for the heart chakra is perfect if you need to ignite or increase empathy, compassion, universal love, self-love, tolerance, patience, gentleness, grace, generosity, selflessness and virtually all the other heart chakra qualities.

You can create a *chi* ball for your sacral chakra to increase your capacity to relate to others. The sacral symbolizes and brings energy to interpersonal relationships, friendships, creativity, joy, self-empowerment relating to social connections, emotions, vulnerability and openness, sensuality, sexual life-force and romance. It is often referred to as the centre for creativity, sexuality and emotions, because it is where these three significant themes tie in. Each sparks the others, and when there are blocks in this chakra or no flow of life-force, each is negatively impacted.

I've mentioned the sacral, heart and third eye chakras here, as these are the ones where psychic gifts originate and flow. But you can also activate your root chakra for security, grounding and belonging, your throat for self-expression and communication, and your crown for cosmic consciousness, faith, purity and divine or angelic contact, if you want to go really high into the spirit realm.

# How to create a *chi* ball

Through this practice, you'll be creating a chi ball for yourself, rather than for the healing of others. *Chi* flows through your body like energy flows through a circuit. Your left hand or palm chakra (yes, there are palm chakras too!) is known as the 'receiver'; your right hand or palm is the 'giver'. (This applies whether you are left or right-handed.)

To make a *chi* ball, you have to come to terms with the idea (and reality) of there being invisible, subtle and spiritual healing energy present in the universe. Then:

- Find a quiet spot where you won't be disturbed and where you feel comfortable, take some deep breaths and get into a meditative space. Set the intention to find silence and peace within, and make sure your breathing is steady.

- Bring your hands up to the level of your heart chakra. Make a cupping motion; your palms should be facing each other an inch or two apart. If you're already an experienced energy healer, you may find your hands naturally fall into place a few inches apart. This is because *chi* grows and expands within your hands, radiating out from your palm chakras.

- Breathe deeply while projecting your intention into the ball of beautiful healing energy growing in between your hands. Project your intentions, while remembering that *chi* flows through all living things and is infinite and always available.

- Visualize – or see – pure white or golden light forming in the space between your palms. If you're making a *chi* ball for a specific chakra, you can visualize a mixture of a golden white light and the colour for that chakra – red for your root chakra, orange for your sacral, yellow for your solar plexus, green for your heart, blue for your throat, purple or indigo for your third eye and simply white for your crown.

- With every inhale, picture this beautiful healing light and energy growing into the shape of a ball between your hands. With each exhale, see more light coming out of your palms and giving energy to the *chi* ball between your hands.

- Start moving your hands in a cyclic motion while keeping your imagery in mind.
- Continue energizing your *chi* ball for at least five minutes and up to one hour if you wish. This is the general rule, but it is advisable to continue for as long as feels comfortable. The average amount of time I would suggest is 10-15 minutes. But start out shorter, if you prefer, and work your way up.
- Once your hands have started to feel a gravitational pull and they have moved further apart, due to the ball of energy growing between them, you will actually be able to feel your *chi* ball circulating. At this point, slowly take the ball to your chosen area.
- Finally, once you feel ready, 'pour' the energy from the ball into or onto your chosen chakra. Watch it spill out and flow into you, filling you with light, love and healing gifts from spirits. Visualize it and feel it happening at the same time!
- Leave it there for a few minutes until you feel silence and peace within.
- To conclude, gently rest the palms of your hands over the chakra, first laying the left palm flat and then placing the right palm over the top of it.
- Keep your hands there for a few moments, feeling the warmth of the healing light flowing through you. At this stage you can say thank you; expressing your gratitude amplifies the flow of positive energy.

- To finish, rub your hands together a few times, as if you are sparking them against each other, attempting to light a fire.
- End by bringing your hands down onto your knees in a meditative position.

## Chakra linking

If you start to feel *chi* balls are your go-to and really work at activating your psychic gifts, you can start to experiment with something known as 'chakra linking'. This is where you make a *chi* ball for two chakras and, when both have been created, 'link' them together.

These are the best combinations for chakra healing:

*Root and heart:* The root and heart are said to link because the root is our sense of grounding and security, while the heart allows the free flow of love and empathy.

*Sacral and throat:* The sacral and throat are said to link because the sacral represents our emotions, interpersonal relationships and capacity for emotional depth and maturity, while the throat is our centre of expression and communication.

*Solar plexus and third eye:* The solar plexus and third eye are said to link because the solar plexus represents ambition and empowerment, while the third eye is the centre for higher cognitive powers, vision and intuition.

*Heart and crown:* The heart and crown are said to link because the heart is where love expands and flows and the crown activates higher cosmic consciousness, in addition to spiritual perception and sight.

## Connecting with nature

- Take a walk outdoors somewhere quiet and peaceful. It doesn't have to be far from home, it could even be your garden, as long as it's somewhere you feel safe.

- I want you now to place your hand on your heart and close your eyes. Take a few deep breaths, and as you do so, imagine a pure light at the top of your head. Allow that light to surround your whole body from head to toe. Imagine this light pouring through your whole body from head to toe, filling every muscle and every cell.

- Keep your hand on your heart and either ask a direct question which you are looking for guidance on, or just ask your intuition to bring what guidance you need to know right now to the forefront of your mind.
- Most importantly, *trust* whatever comes to you first. The message that does should feel as though it has come from your heart and not your mind.

# Connecting with friends and family

- Start your morning by thinking of someone you are likely to see or speak to during the day. It could be a friend, family member or co-worker.
- Bring an image of that person to the forefront of your mind, and once you've done that, take a moment to ask yourself, 'How is this person feeling today?' In reply, you should receive a thought, image or feeling.
- Don't forget to write down what you thought, felt or saw, and see if it comes to light during the course of the day, as it most likely will! This will lead to you starting to trust your intuition more.
- Alternatively, you needn't wait for the proof to emerge, but can just connect with the friend, family member or co-worker and ask how they are feeling.

# Tuning into your Higher Self

This exercise is great for finding out what message(s) your Higher Self has for you. You will need a pen and paper for this one.

- Start by finding a comfortable and quiet space and closing your eyes. Focus on your breathing, and with every breath you take, allow your body to relax from head to toe.
- Imagine the most beautiful light at the top of your head, and imagine pulling this light down from the top of your head into your entire body. As the light washes through you, allow every muscle to become lighter and a feeling of peace and relaxation to come over you.
- Once you feel your mind is clear, open your eyes.
- With your pen to paper, think about something that you would like guidance on, then soften your hand and allow it to write. Try to not think about it too much, as by doing so you will stop any messages from coming through to you. You may need to do this a few times if nothing comes through clearly for you the first or second time.

# Connecting with your intuition before sleep

- Ensure you are fully relaxed after your day. You can do this by meditating for a few minutes prior to going to bed, if you wish.
- Once you are lying in bed, close your eyes and mentally ask your intuition for a dream or image that will benefit your life and the lives of the people around you. You may repeat the request as often as you like before you drift off.
- When you wake up, if there is anything on your mind, write or draw whatever it is, as there will likely be a message or guidance for you within it.

## Being aware and present

To have a clearer connection with our intuition, we must become more present, tune out all distractions and pay more attention to how things look and feel around us.

If you practise doing this, you will become far more sensitive, and your mind will become less clouded by your own distracting thoughts and more open to your intuition. Try the following exercise:

# Being aware and present

- Choose the room that you feel most relaxed in. Settle down comfortably and look at every little detail of that room, from the paint on the walls to the items and décor in there.

- Tune into memories associated with the items in your room. Is there something sentimental from your childhood? Does something spark a memory of a happy, sad, challenging or ecstatic time? Was there a powerful lesson connected to that intense emotion? Is there perhaps something you need to let go of due to painful memories, negative feelings, unhealthy attachment, nostalgia or materialistic-hoarding? (All of these are a reality for many of us!)

I see intuition as a gift from the universe. It is the roadmap that helps us to navigate through situations in our lives, it is the pull within our heart that guides us through life. By listening to your intuition, you are building trust in the one person you will always have with you, and that is yourself.

# 3

# SPIRITUAL AWAKENING

Have you ever suddenly questioned your own beliefs? Questioned your life purpose? Or felt as though you've woken up from a dream and started to see that there is much more to life than yourself and the present moment? If so, you may have experienced a 'spiritual awakening'.

## Notable Events

During a spiritual awakening you may experience transformations in your life. It may be a challenging time when you feel you could be close to giving up. But you will probably find that your sense of purpose and direction becomes much clearer and you will develop a deeper connection to your own self, to others and to the spirit realms.

You may experience intense insights, spiritual experiences and a new connection to the universe and everything around you. You may start to prioritize your own beliefs and values and pull away from anything that does not truly resonate or align with you. You may also develop a heightened sense of empathy and compassion for other people. You may become more aware of your own thoughts and actions, as well as those of others. You may also be inclined to explore spiritual practices such as yoga and meditation.

All or any of these things may happen and it is important to remember that our journey in life is personal and unique and there are never any rules when it comes to our own spirituality. Just be kind, patient and loving with yourself in order to keep your vibrations as high as possible and not fall into negative thought patterns and toxic energies.

This is especially important, because if you have experienced a spiritual awakening, you will know how overwhelmed, lost and confused it can make you feel. Those who experience such an awakening may feel very disconnected from themselves. It almost feels as if you have taken a layer away and become a new person. You may no longer be interested in things that used to fascinate you, your diet may change, your routine may change, but you should feel refreshed and renewed and have a sense of deep inner peace.

Spirituality can mean different things to different people, of course, but it normally involves a belief in something that is available to everyone and also greater than and more powerful than we are. So, during a spiritual awakening you may come to believe that there is something more to being human than what you experience through your senses in the physical world.

In short, notable events you may experience during a spiritual awakening could be any of the following:

- ☐ You may feel disconnected or detached from things, people, places or situations you once prioritized or cared about.
- ☐ You may feel a heightened sense of intuition and be able to sense dishonesty, lies or deceit easily. You may have a heightened 'gut feeling' when you connect with new people.
- ☐ You may change your daily routine or lifestyle and prioritize things you may never have included in your day-to-day schedule before.
- ☐ You may feel that your spirituality or beliefs are far more important to you than before.
- ☐ You may feel more of a connection to nature and the world around you.

Spiritual awakenings can be caused by many different things – life-changing events such as the loss of a loved one or the ending of a relationship, for example. Anything of that nature could create a change in your life energetically, which could bring you to experience what some would see as a spiritual awakening.

Personally, I had my own spiritual awakening when I first experienced the loss of a significant loved one, and that was my grandfather, who passed away when I was 18 years old.

From the moment he passed and throughout the months following, I felt as though my beliefs had changed, as I began to question what happened to a loved one when they died and where they might go. I felt the limiting beliefs that had been embedded in me since childhood fade away as I sought guidance from those within the spiritual fields. They reassured me that my granddad was at peace and that he was still with me, and that helped me through my grief.

My life changed the moment he passed, and I knew I had to do something to make him proud. He wasn't a religious man in any way, and he didn't understand my abilities either, but he believed in me and accepted me.

I was in the early days of developing my mediumship when he passed away, and soon after, he came to visit me. I woke up one night and saw him sitting on the bed beside me. I could see him in fine detail, right down to the tattoos on his arms, and as I moved the quilt cover, thinking I was going crazy (as I often have over the years), he disappeared. I remember going back to sleep feeling as though it was a dream, and it wasn't until the next day that I remembered what had happened. It brought me a great sense of comfort and peace, as I knew he was safe and content, wherever he

SPIRITUAL AWAKENING

was. I also just knew from that moment that he was with me and always would be. I have always seen him as a guide and I feel his influence and support in everything I do.

I am often asked whether a loved one in spirit will come to speak to us if we don't believe in mediumship, and the answer is 'yes'. A loved one will always want to come forward and pass messages to their family and friends.

This leads me to say that we each have not only guardian angels, but also loved ones who watch over us and take care of us, whether we knew them when they were alive or not. How do we get in touch with them? Through extra-sensory gifts and mediumship.

51

# 4

# EXTRA-SENSORY GIFTS AND MEDIUMSHIP

If you wish to progress from developing your psychic powers to something more advanced, such as developing mediumship to connect with spirits and passing on messages from departed loved ones, you'll need to hone your extra-sensory gifts. What are these?

## Extra-sensory Gifts

### The four clairs

The four clairs are the foundational parts of your psychic and intuitive gifts. These are:

*Clairvoyance:* the gift of clear sight or seeing
*Clairsentience:* the gift of clear feeling (like empathy)

*Clairaudience*: the gift of clear hearing
*Claircognizance*: the gift of clear knowing and instinct

Let's explore them further...

## Clairvoyance

Clairvoyance is the gift of clear sight, heightened intuition and the ability to perceive subtle spiritual energy. It equates with an active third eye chakra – the chakra of vision. The practical implications of this are that you can use the wisdom, ancient knowledge and higher perspective accessed via your third eye to help others. This is how you make the most of your psychic and intuitive gifts, by embodying an elevated level of empathy, higher self-awareness and the spiritual wisdom to heal and help.

Accessing dream states and subconscious wisdom are linked to clairvoyance. People with this gift often dream vividly, even lucidly. Lucid dreaming is when you are in your waking-mind state in your dreams, so you can explore the dream space consciously, with partial or full conscious memory upon waking. You essentially have the freedom to 'journey' through multiple dream worlds and dimensions. In fact, there's a vast dream space to explore when you activate the powerful gift of clairvoyance. Clear sight or vision allows you to perceive symbols and imagery, as well as the spirits of those who have died, or living people still in this world, making themselves known to you in the dream space.

In addition, clairvoyant people are aware of things most people miss when meeting others, things like hidden insecurities, fears, health issues, ailments, imbalances, weaknesses, past pain and trauma and personal histories, and also talents, blessings, successes, fortune, gifts, powers and strengths.

Uncovering truth is key to this psychic ability. Clairvoyants can uncover hidden truths on both a personal and collective level. It is quite difficult to lie to them, as they can see the truth. Deception and manipulation can be sensed a mile off, and clairvoyant people can also know when good or bad things are about to happen to someone, or when someone new is about to enter their life.

A clear example of being clairvoyant is thinking of someone for no reason, and your rational or logical mind not being able to explain it, and then, moments later, that person walks into the room. Or they call or text you, or send you a message or email, or you hear a significant story about them in conversation. You may literally 'see' what's happening in their life with your physical eyes, yet the sensation arises below the surface – you're seeing with your third eye.

Seeing auras and swirls of energy is also possible with this clair, as is having imaginative and artistic visions.

## Clairsentience

Clairsentience is clear feeling, the ability to feel exactly what it's like to be in another person's shoes. Clairsentience is the foundation of all other psychic gifts. It can lead to mind-reading, feeling other people's emotions and experiencing subtle energies on multiple planes through direct physical sensations.

Clairsentience is a beautiful gift because it connects you to the world of spirit, the infinite dimensions linked to sensuality, soul and sensitivity. People often report feeling Archangel Michael, and angels, light beings and spiritual entities existing on different planes. This is an intuitive feeling and instinctive knowing. (*More on Archangel Michael on page 219.*)

Psychics, mediums and intuitives always serve from a space of love. Their heart chakras are active and integrated, so they live from a space of heart-mind-body *feeling*, not just thinking. This is key.

Feeling requires emotional intelligence, instincts and soul activation – an awakening of your multi-dimensional self. In this day and age, there's so much emphasis on logic, reasoning, intellect, rationality and a competitive mindset. To be a real psychic or medium, you must go beyond this and use your right brain. This is where intuition flows, coupled with psychic powers, as well as the heart–brain link essential for such powers.

Developing a strong and healthy heart chakra is key for this. You will never find a true psychic, intuitive or medium without an open heart chakra. It's actually impossible to be one without an integrated and strong heart chakra vibration. So, what are the qualities of the heart? Here's a quick reminder:

- Empathy, compassion and nurturing
- Sensitivity
- Kindness, generosity and selflessness
- A genuine desire to help others and serve with love
- Good intentions, purity and warmth
- Benevolence, self-love, unconditional/universal love and humility
- A respect for self, animals and nature

I'll say it again: true psychics work from the heart. We use clairsentience, as well as our other gifts, to genuinely care for others.

## Clairaudience

One psychic power not yet explored is the wonderful gift of clairaudience. Clairaudience is the ability to hear things from other dimensions, planes and realms. You can receive messages through sound, speech and music; these are sounds that you know aren't coming from the physical space around you, but from elsewhere.

Common occurrences include hearing a loved one's voice, such as that of a mother or grandmother, either still alive or on another plane, and hearing bells and chimes. More specifically, many people with psychic gifts hear a bell of a unique frequency that sounds as though it's coming directly from the archangel realm itself ... and it is. It's very real, and it's a global phenomenon for awakening souls destined for a spiritual or healing path.

Hearing angelic voices, and even your own voice, is common. The latter comes from an alternative dimension or future or past timeline of yours. It's your past or future self 'projected' into space, into the Ether, so your message reaches you at the perfect time. Essentially, it's a message from your Higher Self, travelling through the space-time continuum. This is the holographic essence that allows messages from your Higher Self and others to travel through multiple planes and realms of existence.

If you're gifted in clairaudience, you'll also be able to hear tones and frequencies beyond and above the normal range of sound waves. The spaces between waking life and the multi-dimensional planes, including the dream and astral planes, are thin, so the range of 'contact' you can have is infinite. With clairaudience, you can receive guidance, wisdom and messages of love from loved ones or spirit guides. In rare cases, you are able to hear a loved one call out when they need help, such as when they are sick or during the final hours or minutes of life.

Hearing music playing is a common clairaudient occurrence which involves heightened telepathy. All aspects of the musical universe are amplified and fine-tuned.

Finally, a person with the gift of clairaudience can communicate with plants and animals, hearing what they say through the energy and vibrations they emit – their thoughts, feelings, subtle energy, etc.

## Claircognizance

Claircognizance, clear knowing, is a powerful inner feeling of knowing something without logic or rationality. It's very common among empaths and psychic mediums. You may receive a sudden insight or flash of knowledge and higher wisdom. Spiritual ideas, truths and concepts might come to you out of the blue, or memories that provide valuable insight and wisdom may arise spontaneously and effortlessly. You may have absolute certainty about events that occurred in the past or will occur in the future, and you are able to recognize when someone or something is dangerous. People lying, or even distorting the truth ever so slightly, can be sensed on an instinctive level.

There's a high level of intuitive and cognitive activity here. Creative genius, musical and artistic inspiration, and extraordinary imagination and intellect are connected to claircognizance. Deep self-awareness and insights into others and how the universe works are also incorporated into this gift.

Psychic downloads, an activated crown chakra, sensing a range of frequencies and 'just knowing' when to act or speak at the perfect time are frequent in those with claircognizance. If you aren't already aware, psychic downloads involve receiving psychic visions and imagery from the higher celestial, ethereal and spiritual realms. They are something many empaths and psychics experience!

Cosmic downloads also come through books, writings, music, introspection, meditation, artistic and sporty outlets, exercise, reading, sleeping and so forth. Virtually every human activity opens a portal or door to higher consciousness perspectives and to internal 'knowings'.

So, with claircognizance, you may know instinctively or through a gut feeling when to say something, offer some advice, share your perspective or wisdom, enter or leave a room, visit a specific place or refrain from speaking. Your soul speaks to you through your body. Perfect or divine timing comes into play here, as you're attuned to a universal clock.

Others may consider you arrogant, ignorant or superior when you display this gift, but you know your feelings aren't coming from your ego, but from a higher power that is aligned to the divine and Great Spirit!

# Mediumship

To be a medium, as already explained, is to make a connection with the spirit world, so when someone has this ability, they can connect with loved ones and friends that have passed away.

I have never believed that the spirit world is a place that is separate from where we are now. I believe that our loved ones who have passed away are always around us and that they watch over us and support us.

From my own experiences of connecting with the spirit world, I can say that our loved ones are close to us. Think about it this way: if you passed away, you wouldn't want to be far away from those you loved, would you? You'd be looking after your living family and friends, supporting them and watching over them.

As a medium, I find that our loved ones in spirit are able to bring us information, which they can communicate to us through feelings, images and emotions. When communicating with a medium, a loved one in the spirit world will often want to show things about their physical life, such as things they loved to do, the way they dressed, what they did for a living, the experiences they had, their personality and personal relationships, so we can recognize who they are and know they are communicating with us. When participating in a mediumship reading, a loved one will want to validate that the medium is acting as a third party by passing on information that only we could know. These can be details or memories that are specific to our relationship with them, for instance.

When it comes to giving a mediumship reading, you may ask a client to look at a photograph of a loved one who has passed, or perhaps hold an item of jewellery they possessed or another of their former possessions. I have often found that this is helpful in building a connection, and certainly in the instances where the client is looking to connect with a particular loved one.

I don't believe that all of us are mediums; I believe that it is something you are born with, and it is very often passed down through families. I believe that my own connection with spirits has been passed on to me that way. I believe it can be passed to you from birth as part of your life's mission. If it's part of your soul's DNA or blueprint, then it's part of your purpose. It's a beautiful but rare gift.

## Signs that you may be a medium

Here are the eight main signs that you may be a medium:

- ☐ You may feel a presence as though someone is with you.
- ☐ You may hear someone is whispering your name even when no one can be seen.

☐ You may walk into a room and feel heaviness, pressure or hot or cold sensations.

☐ You may recall seeing the spirits of deceased family members at a young age or perhaps you knew about or spoke about people who had passed before you were born.

☐ You may have had imaginary friends when you were young.

☐ You may just know things about people that you have absolutely no way of knowing. Intuition and empathy are precursors to mediumship skills.

☐ You are very sensitive to emotions, you can feel sadness, fear, happiness or anxiety that is not your own, and you may not be sure of where it has come from.

☐ You may have received visitations in your dreams from deceased loved ones or dream characters who seemed to be real souls, spirits from another dimension or world, people from waking life who had passed over.

In the early days of developing my mediumship, I found that it was comforting to sense my own loved ones, and I know that developing mediumship can be so healing for our own grief and loss. It may be something that you would like to develop or it may be something present in your own family that is encouraged. I believe that if you are sensitive and in tune with spirits, then that mediumistic ability will never leave you; it is something that will be with you for all of your life.

In addition to the above signs, there are other signs that you may be a natural medium. These are considered 'advanced signs'.

## Unexplained phenomena

Unexplained phenomena can include hearing voices, seeing apparitions or seeing angelic orbs. Orbs can be in the form of ancestral, angelic, light or spirit guide orbs and can appear as messengers. You may also be receiving messages through clouds, billboards or posters, or through random songs played at key moments. You are aware of them because your subconscious mind is attuned to a different frequency, a frequency other humans miss.

Objects may move or you may see swirls of colour or actual sound waves before or during sleep. This is common for natural mediums. If you are one, your astral body will be very active and awakened. Due to advanced and incredibly evolved extra-sensory powers of perception, you will be able to see the elements and colour and sound frequencies in a way similar to animals, just like dogs hear sounds we can't and dolphins communicate through supersonic waves.

Seeing ghosts or spirits is a clear sign you are a medium. Seeing ghosts is rare, so if you always found yourself seeing spirits as a child, no matter where you went or whose house you stayed in, you are surely a medium. Perhaps they even followed you, in an energetic sense! Did you seem to see and hear people who had passed over in every house you slept in, while other people weren't aware of them? And over 99 per cent of the time, did you feel comforted rather than afraid?

To add to this, you may have always instinctively felt you wanted to help spirits. Without training or qualifications, perhaps you knew on a deep and intuitive level that you had the gift, just like I did. I knew from a young age that I had a calling to do something different, I had a purpose, a message to share with the world. You, too, may have always been sensitive to these souls and drawn to helping them move into the next life. It's an instinct, a feeling, an inner knowing. It's likely you couldn't explain it rationally, but you knew you had the skills of a medium or spiritual healer. It felt like your purpose, a soul calling – an intuitive request from both the spirit world and your Higher Self.

You may have even tried to communicate in some way with the spirits you saw, or simply sent them love and healing, knowing that your loving intentions would help them. You may not have been a professional medium, but you may have acted like one! At least in the sense of communicating with and helping stuck spirits move on to a different realm.

Other unexplained phenomena may have included objects moving at night or crystals randomly appearing or disappearing. You would have been drawn to crystals, of course. Do you know that it's said that they disappear or break when you no longer need them? There is likely to have been at least one occasion when a special crystal entered or left your life at the perfect time.

How does this happen? Crystals are attuned to our vibration and they each emit unique and specific healing frequencies. So, having one for a set period means that in some cases you no longer need that crystal once that period of your life comes to an end. Its healing powers have already done their job. This is when a crystal 'disappears' without logical explanation. You may have intended to keep it with you, but the spirit realm had other plans, so they removed it from your life to show you that you no longer needed its energy.

## A connection to the death-rebirth cycle, afterlife and universal laws

You may have had instinctive knowledge from a young age of how everything in the universe involves death and rebirth, everything restarts or refreshes itself, everything has a beginning and an end, and everything must go round again, returning to its original source. A seed becomes a tree to become a seed again. A relationship ends for one or both parties to regain their independence and move on, maybe into another relationship. The universe expands and contracts into itself, then starts expanding once again. The death–rebirth cycle is present in all things, sentient beings and deities of nature.

As well as being naturally aware of this cycle, people gifted in mediumship tend to have a deep familiarity with past lives, karmic cycles and karmic energies. You may have intuitively felt you were connected to animals or people in past lives and you share a deep and ancestral or celestial bond. You may feel that you have many soulmates in this life, from family and friends to lovers and strangers. Sometimes a connection can be deeper with someone you've known for a few minutes than someone you've known for years.

You instinctively know that you share a deep bond with many people, and it has transcended time and space. This could be linked to karmic exchange, which is the awareness of soul contracts. Not everyone is aware of or even open to the idea of soul contracts, yet they're very real. I believe we each come into this life with many soul contracts, people we are bound to through all time and space and multiple lifetimes.

We are all ancient beings, so someone who may be a lover in this life could have been your mother or best friend in a past life, and vice versa. You may have mistaken a Platonic soulmate for a romantic or sexual one, or vice versa, only to learn the lesson one, three or twelve years later. Your soul contract with someone might be, for example, to finally learn the lesson that they are not a lover, they are only meant to be a friend and someone you share Platonic love with. You may have even spent years in karmic cycles believing something to be true when it was, in fact, an illusion.

The purpose of soul contracts is to transcend cycles from previous lives and this current life that have kept us trapped in toxic cycles! Karma involves a certain level of toxicity, which includes the shadow self, the wounded and unhealed parts of our personalities and souls, otherwise we wouldn't be accumulating negative karma.

Being connected to spiritual insight as well as a higher power enables us to see, feel and experience the subtle energetic exchanges involved in karmic and soul contracts.

## Karma

Karma is the exchange of energy entered into when we send out an intention, so we have many karmic exchanges throughout life. Karmic energy being returned can be as simple as the result of telling a white lie: because we've told one, we're told one by someone else, either later on in this life or in the next. This is a minor example, but the same applies for bigger acts, and can be played out over longer cycles - karma has no time-scale. It can show itself through lessons in love or business repeating themselves, or continuing toxic cycles, negative behaviour and self-destructive activities that hurt ourselves or others. That being said, we can also accumulate positive karma in our lives as long as our intentions are pure and we're not simply acting in order to gather good karma.

Karmic lessons and cycles are there to elevate us, to teach us things about our deepest selves, souls, personalities, strengths, dislikes, likes, follies or shadow traits and various other inner influences. To be aware of them shows we are in tune with our soul, which is what leads to advanced spiritual abilities.

If you are a natural medium, you may also possess a deep understanding of the spiritual realm, how the universe works and the interpersonal exchange between humans, nature and animals.

In addition, you could have very well had the sensation of knowing, without rational thought or explanation, that someone you met was a reflection of you, a perfect mirror. I believe we meet people for a reason, we connect with people for a reason, and we can learn from one another.

You may be surprised to know that not everyone is familiar with such realities. If this is something that has always rung true for you, it's a clear sign you have some medium-istic abilities.

## Visions and premonitions

Visions and premonitions will also come to you. Visions can either be random or the result of an intention, through sitting in meditation and tuning into your Higher Self, for example. Premonitions can show remarkable foresight into a future event or timeline.

The important thing is why, how and what: why do we have visions, how can we strengthen this gift and what exactly is occurring? Let me explain this to you.

### Why do we have premonitions?

First, we have visions and premonitions to show ourselves and others that such gifts are real. Angels and archangels, other celestial light beings and our spirit guides and ancestors want us to evolve and ascend as a species. Spiritual powers are linked into this. The more we evolve and ascend on an individual level, the more others can too, and therefore the better chance there is for humanity to ascend as a whole.

I believe that there are two timelines: a timeline of *fear* and a timeline of *love*. The timeline of fear involves separation, hatred, ego, envy, blame, shame, guilt, violence, jealousy and the evil and toxic acts we see in the world. The timeline of love involves unity, grace, empathy, selflessness, kindness, generosity, compassion and unconditional love.

Being in denial of, closed off from or ignorant of psychic powers puts us on the timeline of fear. We can't ascend to a loving vibration or unified timeline, as we are too concerned with fears, insecurities and judgements – the things that separate us. This keeps our vibration low and also diminishes our gifts and talents.

The timeline of love, on the other hand, sparks divinity, higher truth and the gifts of psychic powers and spiritual healing, and the spirit guides and ancestors that are sent to heal us are able to shine. Each choice, no matter how big or small, that aligns us with the love timeline activates and awakens our hidden psychic powers. This can be as simple as choosing to stop on our path and help someone or give one pound to a homeless person, or choosing empathy and selflessness over ego and selfishness in any given moment. We are often presented with the choice to become conscious of our actions, energy and intentions, and we have choice in whatever we do.

Small acts and deeds contribute to the larger vision of our souls, and therefore our planet. Each of us is just one small wave or ripple in a vast ocean, but each ripple contributes to the ocean. So, know that it all starts with you. You're not insignificant, and your choices aren't either.

Your psychic gifts, including visions and premonitions, will become stronger and more vivid as you continue to align with love and kindness. This has both a personal effect and affects the world as a collective. And, as you must be aware, the more you contribute to global well-being without wanting anything in return (transcending self-serving notions and the desire for personal gain), the more you receive. It's a natural law based on frequency.

In essence, visions and premonitions can become the basis for healing and health on multiple levels, bringing us unity, compassion and universal love in multiple dimensions.

*How can I strengthen my visionary gifts?*
The full answer to this question is given throughout this book, so let's just look at the methods here:

- Visualization, meditation and mindfulness
- Art, nature, music and animal therapy (I'm a huge animal person!)
- Sound healing, shamanic drumming, sound circles and dance activities
- Yoga, kundalini yoga, *tai chi* and other movement practices
- Lucid dreaming, journalling, going within yourself
- Fasting, water and fruit detoxes and cleansing rituals and routines
- Seeing a psychic, astrologer or Tarot reader
- Reading books or listening to podcasts on the spirit world, metaphysical and spiritual studies, the healing arts, health and alternative/holistic medicine

- Detaching from technology and spending time in nature
- Releasing yourself from toxic and karmic cycles, cord-cutting, removing negative entities/dark timelines (including people, places and things)

### What is the purpose of visionary gifts, what can they be used for?

Helping and healing others is the main purpose. Foreseeing future events can help so many people, but only when they ask for your assistance.

I am often asked, 'Do you ever read for someone in the supermarket?' The answer is: 'No.' It would be intrusive to approach someone with information without their request. It is not OK, from a professional standpoint, to give unsolicited advice and readings. Boundaries work both ways – just as you wouldn't want someone to invade your space, you shouldn't force yourself on others. Your angels, guides and spiritual team would advise against it, as would I and other experienced professionals.

Apart from the effect on your reputation, spiritually it's detrimental to both you and the people you're trying to help. Why? Because if someone isn't open to your wisdom, healing or counsel, this creates a block inside them. Giving advice would be like trying to push two of the same polarities of a magnet towards each other; it would only create tension and resistance, despite the sheer effort involved. I would suggest your time, love and energy would be better spent helping those who ask for your guidance.

Seeking out the assistance of a psychic is a request, an active contract and a promise of participation, so only being of service when people directly request assistance not only allows you to receive for your efforts, but also increases your own spiritual life-force and psychic vibration. When someone approaches you, you are repaid with love, respect, money, time and good intentions. When you offer without a willing and open recipient, you receive negativity, dislike and even hate or psychic attack. People can be stubborn or in denial – it's just human nature.

Only giving readings when asked is one of the fundamental teachings of mediums, healers, psychics and spiritual teachers, as what right does anyone have to do or say something that could alter another person's entire life, destiny or timeline? Of course, when faced with a life or death situation, either on the physical level or when there's a situation that you sense could lead to psychological or emotional damage, always trust your intuition and gut instincts, while tuning into your heart and Higher Self to see what the best course of action is.

To be a psychic medium is to be a healer, yet to heal is to restore wholeness and harmony, not to take on the responsibility for another person's healing journey. We all have our own destinies to play out. As a psychic, your job is to know what insight to provide, when and to whom.

## Electronics or technology going crazy in your energy or your home

Another sign that you may be a medium is that electronics, technology and devices malfunction around you. They may even break down altogether. You may find yourself having to replace your phone or laptop every few months, or never being able to get a television channel to work, while other people do it effortlessly, and right in front of you! Sometimes it seems impossible to get things to function. Why? It's your energy field, it's your aura. Psychics, mediums and intuitive healers have a very powerful energy field. Their intentions to heal and radiate love, warmth and kindness are so strong and integrated that they affect everything around them, including inanimate objects. Things break, lights flicker, the fan speed changes, radios start on their own and Wi-Fi doesn't work the way it should.

Yet in some ways, disconnecting isn't a bad thing. Technology, specifically the news and social media, can completely absorb us and disconnect us from our personal reality. The news promotes a lot of fear, hate, ignorance and negativity, while social media circulates toxic projections, hate speech, envy, jealousy and a separation mindset. It fuels ego, hate and disconnection, and doesn't promote unity or connection in the way a heart-centred and conscious community of people does. There's a certain level of unconsciousness associated with both social media and the news; we unload, spill and get sucked into destruction, chaos and drama that we just do not need. If it weren't for these sources, we wouldn't know about certain things, and yet because of these sources, our lives and minds can become filled with negativity.

Other people's personal stories can be enticing, as can global agendas, and, due to the effect that technological interference has on our energy fields, very destructive. Our minds are drawn into a destructive illusion, while our bodies are absolutely polluted by disruptive and negative thoughts. Because of this, the mind, body and spirit connection and the harmony we need are diminished. We become locked into an illusion or distorted frequency, psychologically, spiritually and emotionally, all the while having our spiritual life-force decreased. Purely on a physical level, electromagnetic pollution from technological devices weakens our intuition and our ability to perceive psychically.

From another perspective, once our intuition, combined with our spiritual life-force, is potent enough, we start to influence the technology around us. Essentially, we become our own conduits for universal energy and create, alter and affect the world around us – we shape reality. If you're born into this life as a natural psychic, you'll find that your energy field is so strong it 'tells' technology what to do. For example, if you're in need of some real emotional healing, but your ego wants to play video games, binge-watch TV while eating junk food or get lost in a social media spiral, your Higher Self will kick in and stop the laptop, phone or computer from working. This is just one example, but I'm sure there are many you can relive and reflect on.

## Vivid dreams, lucid dreams and astral projection and travel

This is another big topic, so grab a cup of tea and listen closely... Other major signs of mediumistic gifts are having vivid or lucid dreams. Also, astral projecting and travelling.

### *Vivid dreams*

The gifts of potent intuition and mediumship extend above and beyond waking life, so in dreams you can communicate with living spirits and those who have passed over, receive divine wisdom and inspiration, revisit forgotten memories that add to self-knowledge, and become aware of universal laws that open your heart and expand your understanding as an intuitive.

### *Lucid dreams*

Lucid dreaming is entering into a lucid state, which means your mind is aware and conscious while you're asleep and dreaming. These dreams are vivid and full of powerful imagery. Healing insights and knowledge flow, often specifically linked to psychic powers. You're fully present in the alternative realities and dream spaces you visit. If you do a lot of lucid dreaming, you can gain mastery over it and control events in the dream. It's been described as being the director of a movie! It may sound like fiction, yet it's very real.

Lucid dreams occur during REM, rapid eye movement, sleep, so take note. You can increase your susceptibility to both astral projection and travel and lucid dreaming for advanced wisdom through the use of binaural beats, crystals, transcendental meditation, conscious fasting or cleansing and visualization exercises. So, these are common practices within the psychic and mediumship community.

### *Astral projection and travel*

Astral projection is the ability to leave your body, an out-of-body experience (OBE) that can be done intentionally or can happen when you're asleep, and project your mind into the infinite spaces of the Ether and consciousness. With astral travel, after leaving your physical body, you travel in your astral body through spiritual planes to receive down-loads, wisdom and potent insights for self-transformation and potentially healing others. It's like swimming, travelling through the multiple dimensions of consciousness. Your mind is aware and conscious on some level, and it's connected to your physical body. So, you enter the dream and astral worlds, then return with vivid memories of your experiences.

All these experiences indicate that you have the gift of medi-umship. If you choose to develop this gift, it is important to know that there is absolutely no danger in contacting the spirit world, and no need to have any fear of it.

It is worth noting, though, that this very often brings your own grief and emotions to the surface. Not only that, but to convey their emotions, loved ones who have passed have to make us feel them as well, which very often can make us far more sensitive and emotional than normal.

With this in mind, we'll turn to connecting with the spirit world now...

# 5

# CONNECTING WITH THE SPIRIT WORLD

When connecting with the spirit world, we have to open our hearts and be willing to receive from this realm. More importantly, as with many areas of our lives, we have to make the connection with positive intentions.

To make sure that you are only connecting with loving spirits, it is important to activate psychic protection. This is because, just like us, those in the spirit world have personalities. (*For more on protection, see 'Intentions and Auric Shielding' on page 111.*) Furthermore, when using psychic tools such as Tarot cards or Ouija boards, you must use discernment to ensure that you are psychically safe.

When I'm connecting with the spirit world, it feels as if the loved one I'm connecting with is very close to me, as though they are in the room with me, so to speak. Sometimes it is just a feeling or a knowing that a loved one is present, but I also see spirits as images or what could be described as imprints in my mind. If I asked you to think about what your mother or father looked like, or what your house looked like, you'd have a clear vision in your mind, wouldn't you? This is exactly how I see spirits.

That kind of connection isn't necessary to have contact with the spirit world, though. Our loved ones in spirit can show us signs in a way of letting us know they are with us. You may feel a tickle on your cheek, or a cold draught around you, or you may just feel that someone is around you. Your loved ones in spirit want to let you know they are with you, but they also may not connect in the way you may naturally expect, so you need to be open-minded when you are connecting with loved ones in spirit or connecting with the spirit world.

It's also important to trust what you feel they're showing or telling you. If you are connecting with the spirit world for another person, tell them exactly what you feel and whatever comes to mind, however random. It may be meaningful to them. Very often, we allow our logic to intervene and over-analyse what we feel, but by doing so, we may change the message.

If you choose to develop your mediumistic abilities, you can begin by following meditation practices to clear your mind, as the clearer your mind, the easier it will be for you to connect with the spirit world.

As you're developing your gift, don't get caught in your head by focusing on what everyone else has experienced.

Remember that we all have our own unique experiences on our journey to mediumship. While there are more common occurrences, there's no single path you can go down to develop your gift.

However, on your own unique path you will meet at least one spirit guide.

## Spirit Guides

I believe that all of us are born with at least one spirit guide. Our guides help us from behind the scenes and often we don't even know they are there; the same goes for our angels. (*More on angels in Chapter 10.*) Both our guides and our angels are here to assist us. Our guides are most likely people that we don't know and have never met, but they have lived many lives and have a lot of experience, wisdom and knowledge that they can bring to us. They always want us to know that they are with us and that they are helping and guiding us. Normally, we are the ones who put up a block or barrier, as we don't believe they are truly there, and this prevents them from coming closer to us.

I do feel that spirit guides play a part in helping us connect with the spirit world, so to have a clearer understanding of how to do that, it is normally beneficial for us to have a connection with our guides first. We all have guides and none of us have better guides than others.

Spirit guides will often make their presence known by sending us signs and synchronicities – meaningful coincidences. Just like with our intuition, when our mind is quiet, we will see the signs and messages that our guides are trying to bring to us more clearly, and the more that we watch for signs from our guides, the more we'll recognize the signs they're sending us. As our guides see that we're aware of them and acknowledging their messages, they'll send more to us.

Make sure that you remind yourself every day that your spirit guides are sending you messages, and you'll become more consciously aware of them. You'll notice the signs more than before.

One of these signs may be a particular number sequence. You might be going for a job interview, for example, and the numbers 111, 222 or even 333 appear. What do they mean?

# 'Angel Numbers'

Angels, loved ones and spirit guides often communicate with us through numbers. We'll see these 'angel numbers' on billboards, on posters, in films, on pieces of paper, on clocks or watches or mobiles and in many other places, and hear them through music, sound, people talking and faint whispers. These are messages straight from the divine and our Higher Self and they serve a variety of different purposes:

- They're here to show us the divine synchronicities all around us. Synchronicity is defined as 'a seemingly random event, meeting or occurrence which shows us the divine and interconnected nature of reality'. There's a real sense of wonder, excitement and inspiration present when we recognize synchronicities - magic too! We feel that nothing happens by chance, because it doesn't - there's a grand design behind everything.
- They show us how far along we are in our awakening or where we're at with our spiritual gifts. The specific meanings of the number sequences we see tell us what our current frequency is, where and how we're vibrating and what our current life trajectory is. They show us our current challenges, setbacks, strengths, weaknesses, destiny, life path and anything else we might need to know.
- They remind us that we're not alone and that we'll always have support on our journey. As numbers are vibrations, unique frequencies, they can be used as channels or conduits. A loved one, guide, spirit animal, ancestor or even deity might send you a message through an angel number. It will always appear at the perfect time, exactly when we need to receive the message or reassurance.

By studying the meaning of angel numbers, we can raise our inner vibration and connect to our intuition.

The most significant angel numbers involve the master numbers 11, 111 or 1111, 22, 222 or 2222, 33 or 333 and 44 or 444. The numbers 55 and 555 are also significant. I would like to share the meaning of these with you because I am certain, as are my guides, that you will come across them on your journey.

## The famous 11:11

When it comes to numbers, everyone asks, 'What is 11:11?' Seeing 11, 11:11 (on clocks or phones) or 1111 is extremely common; in fact, it's a universal phenomenon.

More than that, 11:11 is a power portal to higher consciousness! It symbolizes evolution, ascension and being on a truly authentic spiritual path. This famous angel number speaks to our soul; it speaks of alchemy, personal awakening, enlightenment and accessing the most advanced spiritual gifts, including intuition, clairvoyance and mediumistic abilities.

Numerologically, 11:11 is a gateway to our Higher Self as well as the angelic and soul planes.

It's incredibly important to be aware of this number when seeking to develop your psychic gifts, unlock your psychic power in harmony with your spirit guides and connect with the spirit world.

Here are some key aspects of 11:11 (or 11 or 1111) that you should know:

## Soulmate and Higher Self synchronicity

Friendships and relationships that serve our Higher Self or divine purpose are strongly indicated here. When we see this number, we are being guided towards community, pathways of unity, solidarity and togetherness, especially when it comes to joining forces with other magicians and high priestesses. In fact, 11:11 is associated with both The Magician and The High Priestess cards in the Tarot (*see pages 159 and 160*), as well as The Hierophant, Empress and Fool (*see pages 162, 160 and 158*). Soulmates coupled with our intimate connection with our own soul serve a greater purpose, and this is the angel message here. These soulmates are here to set us on new paths of awakening, soul and spirit contact and divine communication, in all its beautiful manifestations.

## A doorway or bridge to cosmic consciousness and our soul purpose

Also, 11:11 is a power portal, a bridge to deeper parts of our soul, psyche and innate intuitive and psychic gifts. It sparks memories from our childhood and past, memories linked to spirit encounters we may have repressed or pushed down.

Society can be very limiting to our souls. It teaches us to be dominant, logical and cut-throat, callous, calculated, or simply intellectual and rational. There's little space for emotional intelligence, instincts, sensitivity, selflessness (the higher manifestation of kindness), community, and cooperation, teamwork and harmony or spiritual energies. Quite simply, society breeds separation, while community gives birth to unity, yet we're not living in a community-based world.

The suppression, even persecution, of soul gifts and talents is very common in our world, and the qualities and abilities necessary to become a medium or psychic aren't often encouraged. They are actually *dis*couraged, being seen as something make-believe, delusional or crazy. You will probably remember the time when psychics, spiritualists or herbalists and the like were perceived as 'crazy'; thankfully we are in a world now that is more open minded and accepting. If we break down the word 'luna-tic', it means a sparking of Luna's energies. Luna is our majestic moon, the planetary body best representing sacred knowledge, feminine wisdom, instincts, intuition and empathic qualities. People were often put in lunatic asylums because they were in touch with spiritual and subconscious powers which sought to undermine the entire system, as well as certain religions.

As an angel number, 11:11 is the most soul-stimulating and higher-consciousness and wisdom sparking. It awakens all the clair gifts, advanced spiritual abilities and repressed or hidden powers in potent measure. It reminds us of what we once knew but have forgotten over time. This links with the next point.

## Letting go of toxic and self-destructive cycles

This angel number is a catalyst to letting go of the past. It asks us to look to our future self, moving from past to future. The past can include outgrown and outdated versions of ourselves, toxic relationships, unhealthy chapters, karmic cycles, any place, object or connection that doesn't serve our future selves. As one of the master numbers, 11 guides us towards our best selves, towards our ultimate vision of our lives, including where we see ourselves, our professions or vocations, our roles and service in the world, and how able we are to move away from our shadows and towards our light.

Every one of us has a light and a dark side. The shadow self is symbolic of our toxic traits, follies and flaws, and to move towards our inner light we must come to terms with it. We can't repress or dismiss our flaws; at some point, we must embrace the darker parts of our souls and psyches to reclaim our spiritual powers.

### Handy tip

Research your North and South Nodes in astrology. These can help you in a major way, as the North Node represents where you are heading: your true path, talents, soul plan, future self and evolution. The South Node is what you are supposed to transcend in this lifetime and leave behind.

## Seeking harmony, teamwork and cooperation

Numerologically speaking, 11:11 brings the energies of the number 2. This number represents harmony, teamwork, cooperation, partnerships, balance, support, empathy, loving-kindness and fairness. This is a big 'companionship' number, symbolizing Platonic, romantic and business partnerships and family bonds. People with life path 2 are incredible nurturers and caregivers with many empathic gifts, in addition to being amazing friends and lovers. They're the support system, essentially, using potent instincts, compassion and imaginative insights to help and serve. Life path 2s are empaths, natural healers and counsellors. The higher vibration of life path 2 is 11, so seeing angel number 11:11 (or even 11) pushes us onto its foundation frequency.

## A life partner aligned to divine consciousness

A real possibility with frequently seeing 11:11 is being destined for a divine partnership aligned to an angelic, spiritual or mutual service-oriented frequency. Soulmates and twin flames come under this angel number.

Essentially, if we seem to see 11:11 everywhere, on watches and clocks, or hear it in songs and other places, we're supposed to have a higher love, which is defined as a lover who shares our mission or purpose or has the same set of talents and gifts.

Moving from 3D love to this '5D' love is intrinsic to angel number 11:11. In short, 3D love may be considered 'karmic love', involving soulmates we meet in youth who perhaps feed some of our demons, while 5D love involves soulmates we meet when we are older and wiser, with much more life experience and perhaps our spiritual self and Higher Self intact.

## Fresh starts, new beginnings and manifestation powers

Angel number 11:11 is also all about fresh starts and reclaiming our sovereignty, independence and autonomy. It's a power portal to innate manifestation powers too. Number 1 is a masculine number representing initiation, dominance, assertion, self-authority, self-empowerment and will-power; it's the first number, which means it provides a direct connection with the Creator, the universe and creative life-force in general. So, 11:11 is about a new beginning with our soul mission, life purpose and spiritual path. Opportunities and infinite potential are keywords here. We can tap into our innate powers to manifest, initiate, create, dominate (with love, of course!) and influence reality.

We live in a world of subtle and spiritual energy. In the words of revolutionary inventor and scientist Nikola Tesla, 'If you want to find the secrets of the universe, think in terms of energy, frequency and vibration.' We can use this energy and work with our angels and spirit team to mani-fest and co-create what we would like to have in our life, whether that's abundance, new relationships, prosperity, love, friendship, educational and professional pathways and so forth.

Number 1 also represents creative and artistic vision, innovation, self-leadership, inventiveness, originality and intuition. Angel number 11:11 and the synchronicity phenomena that accompany it are symbols for the mind, body and spirit connection. You may be thinking, 'Isn't the Holy Trinity associated with number 3?' You would be correct. But, as the first masculine number linked to conscious powers of creation and manifestation, 11:11 (four times the power of 1) does ask us to become aware of our mind, body and spirit connection.

## Moving away from negative/bad karma

Finally, 11:11 brings a strong 'past to future' energy, which, when we look deeper, we can see means transcending negative karma. Number 1 is associated with Aries, the first sign of the zodiac, which is concerned with winning and coming first and can be embodied by the fiery and courageous warrior with a strong egotistical side. Positively, Aries is determined, ambitious, innovative, intuitive, intelligent and powerful. Yet it's also egotistical, bullying, over-powering and rather brutal. Those born under this sign can be too concerned with competition, outshining others and being the best, which accumulates a lot of negative karma. The same attributes, both positive and negative, are common with life path 1 individuals. Numerology and astrology influence all of us here on Planet Earth. Thus, seeing angel number 11:11 on our path asks us to move away from negative karmic influences in our life.

A simple way to do this is to reflect on your past deeds and actions, things that may have pulled you off-centre, misaligning you with a righteous or divine path. Have you acted or spoken with less than pure, kind, holy, righteous, helpful, empathic, sincere, honest intentions? We all have! But bad karma is only accumulated when such acts are carried out with ill wishes and malicious intent. Being a good and kind person with a pure heart and spirit breeds good karma.

There's no black or white, just shades of grey, but some of us are more geared towards our inner devil rather than our inner angel, or vice versa. If you wish to receive the best guidance and healing from angel number 11:11 and the other 1s, examine your past. Words, actions and above all intentions are what creates good or bad karma.

Always remember you can research the actual qualities of life path 11, the master intuitive and illuminator!

To save you time, here they are in a nutshell:

# Life path 11

Life path 11 is:

- Highly intuitive, instinctive and gifted in the four clairs
- Incredibly imaginative with unique artistic, musical and visionary gifts
- Multi-talented, open-minded, philosophical, wise beyond their years and seer-like
- A natural healer, psychic, shaman, medium, energy worker, channel, mystic and master of esoteric and ancient wisdom and sacred law
- Sensitive, super-empathic, nurturing, teamwork- and harmony-focused, humanitarian, altruistic, universally compassionate and loving
- Spiritually advanced, a spiritual illuminator, diplomatic, a peacekeeper and a justice-bringer concerned with universal and higher truths
- Visionary, charismatic, inventive, original, independent and idealistic, with powerful speaking, healing and teaching skills

Life path 11s are amazing storytellers too.

## 22:22: The master manifestor

The second of the potent angel numbers you will almost certainly see once you begin to awaken your psychic gifts is 22 or 22:22. The second of the master numbers, 22 is the number of strong physical foundations, practicalities and self-mastery in the following skills: creating order and structure, organization and forging stable and secure material foundations for spiritual and creative life-force to flow.

The foundation of the angel numbers 22 or 22:22 is number 2, the number of harmony, relationships, partnership, a nurturing and empathic spirit and taking on a caring and supportive role. So, if we take this nurturing and peace-keeping foundational vibration and apply it to this master number, we can see that 22:22 is the master builder, creator and forger. Seeing this angel number on your path is a sign that you should be forming sustainable, prosperous and co-creative partnerships. You may already be a master builder, blessed with incredible practical powers of foresight and responsibility, and a visionary.

Angel number 22 brings the qualities of vision, idealistic thinking, dependability and trustworthiness, and the ability to create harmony and peace and gain a deep understanding of self. Self-knowledge, ancient wisdom and the Laws of Attraction, Order, Vibration, Cause and Effect are also linked to angel number 22. (*For more on the universal laws, see Chapter 8.*) In addition, seeing this number indicates we have the capacity to give professional advice coupled with practical wisdom rooted in empathy, sensitivity, caring, nurturing, compassion, diplomacy, fairness and sincerity. The number 2 is a deeply diplomatic, selfless and feminine number, while 22 is symbolic of mastery of these gifts combined with practical wisdom.

Seeing this angel number on our path is a push towards devotion and discipline, getting real with finances, domestic issues, responsibilities, duties and professional goals, in harmony with our spiritual purpose.

## 333: Christ consciousness

Angel numbers 33 and 333 are known as the Christ consciousness numbers. These are the numbers best symbolizing Christ, Krishna, unity consciousness, higher consciousness perspectives, higher truth, divine and spiritual laws and self-empowerment. Personal presence, coupled with self-awareness, is at the core of 33 and 333. These are the synchronicity numbers that guide us to spiritual awakening and illumination, enlightenment, and divine and ancient wisdom. There's a feeling of awakening and *déjà vu* when we see 33 or 333; many people report a sensation of awakening from a dream, as if this physical reality is a construct and not real. This is because it isn't! Consciousness, ideas and knowledge from our psyches and the realm of thought, emotion and inner spirit give rise to physical reality as we know or perceive it.

Angel number 333 asks us to activate healing and spiritual and divine gifts, as well as psychic and intuitive ones. Three is also the number of the Holy Trinity, or mind, body and spirit, which signifies how we can understand and establish a divine connection. Imaginative, musical and artistic gifts are either available to us when we see 333, or we are being guided to embrace these.

Live up to your full potential when you see this number! You hold unlimited power; the unlimited and infinite power of the universe is available to you with 333. You can be in touch with heavenly and celestial forces, such as archangels, Christ, Krishna and any other deities you believe in. The number 33 symbolizes Buddha and enlightenment, while 333 is a symbol of Christ (and Krishna) consciousness.

Starting to see 33 or 333 is a sure sign we have a greater destiny in store for us, a soul mission and a spiritual life purpose. We may be destined to create or contribute to a legacy as a healer, musician, artist, teacher, lecturer, speaker, inventor, scientist, environmentalist, humanitarian, visionary or spiritual leader. The key qualities of these numbers include self-expression, optimism, innovation, originality, intelligence, commitment to universal and higher truths, clairvoyance, faith, hope, inspiration, a love of divine law and order and following our highest joy.

Angel number 333 is a call for authenticity, self-awareness and stepping into positions of leadership and responsibility. A higher sense of service, as well as duty and a desire to heal and help others, on both a personal and planetary level, is key to this number. It also represents diplomacy, justice, cooperation, fairness and becoming a peacekeeper and harmony-bringer in a family, social, business, group or community setting. It's the number of self-mastery, so if you keep seeing this, you are likely to be destined for greatness! This could be in your creative work, healing or any other service or business.

Spirit guides and helpers work closely with angel numbers 33 and 333, because these are the ones closest to God and the spiritual realm. Expect to see 33 and 333 on your path if you haven't already, as these are your keys to awakening.

## 444: Potent manifestation

The numbers 44, 444 and 4444 are powerful numbers directly from the angels! If you keep seeing them, your angels and spirit team want you to know that you are seen, supported and cherished. You have endless emotional, practical and financial support, if you are open to receiving it. You should be receptive and open at this time, even vulnerable.

As the number 4 brings the energy of practical foundations, order, structure, organization, discipline and a high level of responsibility, duty and service, angel numbers 44 and 444 are those of practical magic. This is a very lucky angel number to see, because it represents higher wisdom and self-knowledge linked to your chosen professional path.

If you are a healer, psychic or medium, or about to become one, this is a great positive sign from your angels! Your spirit guides are telling you to direct your attention towards inner strengths and practical matters, as well as security measures and self-discipline. It is a call to be devoted to your path or profession, without fear or self-doubt.

Letting go of pessimistic thinking, coupled with low self-esteem from past lovers, family members or enemies, is key to angel number 44/444. This number represents devotion of the highest order, a dedication and commitment to our life path and purpose. We're being guided to merge creating and seeking structure and security with strong foundations for creative, spiritual and healing gifts to flow.

This angel number also points to powerful manifestation abilities, instincts and physical vitality. It generally means we are becoming more self-reliant and self-sufficient, and its message is that now is the time to work hard, save and make a plan for the future, while seeking structure and order.

Seeing 44/444 also means that it is time to cultivate the qualities of determination, modesty, humility, integrity and selflessness. The number 44 is a deeply selfless one concerned with service to others. There's innate knowledge of sacred law and order here too. The angel message is: 'Be determined, persevering and dedicated. Live with grace combined with a sense of purity, and try to balance and harmonize logic and analytical thinking with instincts and feeling.'

Both practical and creative inspiration are available to us when we see this angel number and it reminds us that we are a channel through which universal energies can flow.

Overall, 44 and 444 are both big blessings, showing us that we can expect divine support, blessings and increased levels of patience, security, self-reliance, resilience, hope and spiritual and material balance.

## 555: The path of freedom

Angel master number 555 is a sign that we should be thinking about our independence. It's a message of sovereignty, independence and autonomy, and points to becoming our own boss. If you have begun to see this number, you are being guided to reclaim your youthful independent and free spirit.

This number points to embracing a passionate path. It's asking, 'What lights up your soul? What is your heart's true desire and greatest joy?' It symbolizes passion, joy, originality, innovation, inventiveness, optimism, intellectual and imaginative power and awareness of the multi-dimensional. When we speak of the multi-dimensional, it's not necessarily something mystical. It can be as mundane as recognizing the different elements that come together to make us a full person, mental, emotional and physical, along with the many aspects of life, such as embracing new cultures and ideologies.

In fact, educational, professional and travel opportunities are synergistic with the angel number 555. It brings the energy of embracing change in life, in one or multiple areas. The number 5 represents change, transformation and personal awakening!

It symbolizes travel and adventure too, so seeing angel numbers 55 or 555 is a clear sign from your spirit guides to be more spontaneous. Perhaps your life path or purpose involves travel or taking regular trips abroad to expand your professional and educational connections. You should try to leave your routines in the past, or at the very least mix up your lifestyle with more travel breaks.

Kindred spirit, romantic and creative connections are another message of this master angel number. There's a strong pull towards being more affectionate, romantic and loving in friendships, business bonds or creative partnerships. There's a desire to merge freedom with innovative solutions to all life problems or setbacks! Embracing infinite potential, welcoming new opportunities, chasing big dreams, realizing goals and combining travel and adventure with professionalism are key to 55/555.

If you keep seeing these angel numbers, it might be part of your destiny to be a digital nomad, world traveller or travelling healer or psychic medium.

An additional meaning of 55 is looking inwards and outwards simultaneously, so when we see this number, we are likely to be introspective and introverted, appreciating self-reflection and taking time to explore the deeper meanings and mysteries of life, while being outgoing, social and extroverted.

Seek out spontaneous and fun-loving connections that serve both your spirit and your professional vocations when this angel number appears! Don't slack or be lazy, and don't give into peer pressure. There are lots of fun and colourful people who aren't going to advocate anti-social behaviour, toxic cycles, and so forth. Seek out inspiration while stepping into pathways that allow you to be inspirational.

Self-leadership is another message and meaning. The numbers 55 and 555 are telling us we have strong personal power and the presence to make waves in our chosen field. We are strong-willed, courageous and fighters for truth and justice.

Attune to a bigger-picture frequency when you see these numbers. Call on your guides and angels for help with any success-oriented or career goals and visions.

Finally, be careful of being impractical and irresponsible. This number does bring the warning of not succumbing to so much joy, freedom and fun that it affects your security or wealth manifestation. Overzealousness is something to be mindful of too...

# Dreams and your Spirit Guides

If you want to connect with spirits, there is no need to have any objects, the only thing you need is your own quiet mind. This is the foundation from which to expand spirit communication. It is easier for spirits to reach us when our minds are calm and quiet, and by setting the intention of wanting to connect with spirits and following basic meditations, we can very easily start to build a connection. Working more consciously with our dreams can help us do this too.

Our spirit guides may actually send us dreams. These could give us an idea about how to handle a situation we feel stuck in, or a guide could even appear to us in a dream.

Also, it is in dreams that we get to explore our darkness as well as the collective or general darkness of life. Dreams are generally considered a dark space, in that the astral and dream worlds, the places we enter when we sleep, are tied into the moon and her subtle influences. In the daytime we absorb the energies and loving rays of the sun, primarily. These are dominant, masculine, light, assertive, active, forceful, direct, electric, yang forces. The moon, on the other hand, brings the energies of receptive, feminine, dark, passive, gentle, magnetic, yin forces. The sun represents the conscious mind in addition to intellectual and mental power. The moon symbolizes the subconscious mind in addition to intuitive, instinctive and emotional power. Thus, the places we enter in sleep are subconscious, unknown to us. They are places of darkness, the unmanifest, the emotions, spiritual and subconscious energies and wisdom – everything that isn't visible in waking life.

That being said, there's a lot of self-knowledge, inspiration and communication from our guides and spirit team to be found in dreams. The dream realm is where we explore our deepest feelings and desires. We can access things we're not aware of in waking life, and there's a lot of hidden power and knowledge in the unmanifest, the unconscious, the subconscious dimensions. I am not a dream worker *per se*, but as a psychic, I am passionate and knowledgeable about the power and importance of dreams.

I mentioned earlier that all you needed for spirit communications was a still and quiet mind and a positive intention, but there are key tools and techniques you can add to the mix to help enhance spirit contact while you sleep.

## How to enhance your ability to receive spirit contact and communication during sleep

Dreams are an opportunity for your spirit team to communicate with you and help you in developing your spiritual gifts. This is because they are a gateway to the astral and soul planes, the two dimensions in which you can explore your gifts and enhance your capabilities.

There are certain things you can do, take or use to amplify your receptivity to advanced dreams and thus spirit contact states:

- Herbal supplements
- Binaural beats, sound mantras and nature therapy music
- Crystals for expanded consciousness

The crystals that are ideal for lucid and vivid dreaming are: amethyst, clear quartz and lapis lazuli. These three are all you need! They will help you explore the vastness of the dream space while increasing lucid, prophetic and spirit contact dreams. (More on crystals in Chapter 6.)

## Opening Up to the Spirit World

When we connect with the spirit world, we are naturally opening our hearts to build an energetic connection, and our thoughts, feelings and emotions normally become replaced by those of spirit, usually the spirit of a loved one who has passed over.

We can access these feelings through seeing, knowing, hearing, smelling, feeling, touching or even tasting. The most common ways are seeing, knowing and feeling. (*See page 52 if you want a reminder of the clairs.*)

Opening up to the spirit world may feel overwhelming, especially when we're quite new to it. It can feel a bit like opening floodgates, more so if we have mediumistic ability but have closed it off all our life.

Over the years working as a psychic, I have met many people who have a fear of spirits or of what may happen if they choose to embark on spiritual development. I must stress that in over ten years of practice I have never had an experience that has frightened me or concerned me in any way. I can understand why you may be scared of inviting spirits or loved ones to connect with you – the unknown can always bring anxiety. But I can say that I personally have always felt very comforted and a sense of peace when working with spirit, or anything psychic. Furthermore, I can assure you that no loved one in spirit would ever want to hurt you or do you any harm.

When I connect with the spirit world, the energy is very content and peaceful. It is as though my own thoughts become quieter and I start to become more aware of my emotions. When I actually connect with a loved one, the whole spectrum of emotions is possible. However, I will say again that I have never felt afraid or had a bad experience, and I can assure you that if your intention is positive then you have nothing to be afraid of.

The importance of intention cannot be stressed enough: when you have positive intent, you will only attract the good that you wish for. You may have heard someone talking about how they have had a bad experience or how they have perhaps dabbled in something which led to them being afraid of spirit, but they probably didn't have the best intentions to begin with.

If you are connecting with a spirit for either your own healing and development, or the healing of another person, then there is absolutely no reason why things should go wrong. Spirits are always willing to make a connection with the aim of helping, healing and guiding.

When starting your connection with the spirit world, it is important to set a clear intention in terms of what it is you are looking to connect for. Is it for your own healing or for the healing of another person? I would recommend saying a simple prayer and carrying out some protection exercises too (*see page 113*). It's important that you feel safe, so that when you do make the connection with spirit, you feel content and calm and no message is scrambled or stopped from coming through to you.

## Finding support in your tribe

I found it very helpful in the early days of developing my psychic gifts and mediumship to surround myself with like-minded people and be around people who were supportive

YOU MUST BE PSYCHIC

of what I believed in. You don't want to have your beliefs pushed away by those who don't believe or haven't awakened to this yet.

Finding support in your tribe or community is the best way to strengthen your gifts and feel reassured and protected. You may have a local elder or master teacher nearby from whom you can receive healing or advice. You should enquire as to whether they offer individual therapies, as having a session with a psychic or medium yourself can open your eyes to the wonderful realms of spirit. There's a lot of inspiration, knowledge and self-empowerment to be gained from visiting an established psychic, whether a Tarot reader, astrologer, Reiki practitioner, sound therapist, shamanic healer, energy worker, holistic body therapist, medium or other psychic or healing practitioner of any kind.

Secondly, you should research events, workshops and courses to spark or strengthen the sensations you're experiencing. It doesn't matter if you're a beginner or highly experienced. That's irrelevant, because a qualified psychic will always have your best interests at heart. They will be aware that it's your journey and you walk your path alone. There is little to no ego present in psychics who have made a name for themselves; they must have ascended on a personal level while gaining a positive reputation. You can't fake this!

Your local energy practitioner or psychic might hold weekly or monthly circles, as is the case in many towns and cities. These are safe spaces in which to explore your own gifts while being supported by others. You give and receive in equal measure. Your tribe empowers you, and you are given the chance to open up in a way that allows you to help and inspire others in turn. I have personally found that local community circles are one of the most effective ways to both practise and explore your gifts. Dormant powers come to light and hidden abilities can be accessed in a compassionate and welcoming environment. There's a lot of love, empathy and consideration in such spaces.

Always trust in your intuition when seeking out events, courses and circles run by practitioners or clairvoyants. I suggest meditating and tuning in to see if they are right for you. As much as I don't advocate judgement, there are cultural aspects that need to be considered. For example, some people may resonate with psychics who embody a strong masculine energy, or those who have been brought up in a certain religion. This religious aspect connects them to the spirit world in a way that feminine and newer generation psychics don't always possess. On the other hand, some people don't like the dogma and traditional views incorporated by older generational healers and psychics and prefer someone in their thirties or early forties who has embarked on a path of healing, yoga and spiritual studies. It is all about whom you personally resonate with. We each have our individual needs and requirements.

There are, of course, other ways to find support in your tribe, such as through online communities, social media groups and magazines or websites that provide support and community forums, opportunities to comment or join video calls, etc. Many authentic psychics, healers and spiritual teachers hold regular Zoom meetings or circles for deeper connection and spiritual communication. We are so blessed in this day and age to be able to connect online, and that is how I initially built my reputation and client base.

## Finding support from your spirit guides

I want to include a meditation for you that will help you in making a connection with your spirit guides if you have never done this before. They are of course an incredible source of support.

I would recommend recording this in your own voice and then replaying it to yourself, as it is incredibly powerful when listening to your own voice.

# Meditation to connect with your spirit guides

In this meditation you are going on a journey to connect with your spirit guides. Sit comfortably, with your feet planted firmly on the ground, and breathe deeply.

With every breath you take, allow your mind and body to relax.

With every breath you take, you are bringing source energy in through your crown chakra at the top of your head.

Imagine a powerful and bright light at the top of your head. This light can be any colour or size. Visualize it filling your entire body, eliminating, worry, fear, anxiety, stress and every other negative emotion.

Moving your focus down to your feet, imagine roots running down from the soles of your feet, planting you firmly in the ground.

As you journey to meet your spirit guides, you need to feel safe and protected, so I would like you to imagine yourself in a cloak of protection. This cloak protects you from any negative thoughts and energies and ensures you are only welcoming in good, positive and loving energy. This cloak will always be around you when you are communicating on a spirit level.

Imagine now that you are walking through the most beautiful garden or landscape. You feel a sense of love and peace here. You are surrounded by natural beauty - trees, flowers and animals. You can see the sun shining, you can feel its warmth on your skin. The sun beats down on your face and you feel completely safe.

As you walk through the garden, you come to a bench. It seems to be a peaceful space, so you take a seat and bask in the sun.

As you look around, you notice a light appear ahead of you in the distance, and it starts to get brighter and brighter. As you focus on it, it comes towards you.

You know that you are not alone here and someone has come to join you, but you feel safe, calm and at peace. A part of you feels that you've known them all along. There is nothing to worry about and no reason to have any fear. You give them permission to come and join you. You are excited to meet them and discover more about them, as you know they have been with you and guided you since the moment you were born.

You are filled with feelings of peace and calm, as you realize you are in the presence of a higher spirit, a guide, a friend who has wisdom to share with you.

As they come closer to you, the light starts to fade, and as it does, you become more aware of whether they are male or female and start to see what they look like and the way they dress.

Say, 'Hello,' and welcome them. Thank them for coming forward to be with you now, and let them know you are so grateful that they have made this connection with you right now.

You are welcome to ask your guide any questions you wish, and as you do so, they will give you the answers, and all you need to do is trust your heart and trust the first thing that comes into your mind.

You may want to ask questions such as 'Am I doing the right thing?' 'What is my purpose?' 'Do you have any guidance for me right now?' or 'What is it that I need to know today?'

When you have received the information you would like to know then you are welcome to let them drift away. If you just thank them and say, 'Goodbye,' they will naturally start to walk away.

You'll see them start to be cloaked in the beautiful light that you saw before and then slowly fade and disappear.

You are back looking at the beautiful garden you saw before, feeling the warmth of the sunlight, the comfort, the sense of well-being, the peace and serenity, and now you are bringing yourself back into the moment, into your own body, so that you are fully aware of all your senses.

You feel both relaxed and calm, and you are going to take this feeling of well-being with you into the rest of your day.

You can return to this garden whenever you wish and know that your guide will always come to you and support and guide you.

# Intentions and Auric Shielding

As empaths, we are constantly absorbing people's energy, whether that energy is positive or negative. Because of this,

I have found setting intentions and protecting myself helpful over the last few years. It keeps me from taking on feelings from outside sources, perhaps people I struggle to be around, busy places, or environments that are stressful or overwhelming, so I am less affected by what others say, do and make me feel.

## Protection

Protection can often give us peace of mind when we are worried about negative energies, perhaps because we have to work with someone we don't get on with, or have to be around someone who is particularly negative towards us. I firmly believe that thoughts are energy (*see page 194 for the Law of Attraction*). Has someone ever said something to you and you've felt it hit you like a curveball to the gut? Pay attention to how you feel when you are around particular people, places or situations, as they can not only affect your mood, but also hinder your connection with your intuition and the spirit world. To be able to connect clearly with our intuition, we need to be mindful of not only what we do with our time, but also whom we spend our time with and how they make us feel.

I believe that everything in this world is energy, so doing protection exercises daily will bring about a change. I often use the following exercises if I am struggling with a particular situation or person, or feeling under the weather or more vulnerable than usual. I feel that when we are slightly under the weather, we may be more susceptible to negative energy.

Here are some very simple exercises which you can practise daily to bring protection into your life when facing negativity from others.

# Cloak of protection

Close your eyes and imagine a bright light at the top of your head. This light can be any colour or size.

As you breathe in and out, imagine this light pouring down over your entire body. As it does, you should instantly feel a sense of calmness and peace wash over you.

I want you now to ask your spirit guides, loved ones or God (or whichever higher power you feel closest to) to place a cloak of protection around you.

As this cloak surrounds you, set the intention of protecting your own energy and space from others' negativity. If something or someone in particular is bothering you, you can set the intention to be protected from the specific situation or person.

# Mirrors of protection

Close your eyes and imagine a bright light at the top of your head. This light can be any colour or size.

As you breathe in and out, imagine it pouring down over your whole body. As it does, you should instantly feel a sense of calmness and peace wash over you.

I want you now to imagine being surrounded by mirrors, and those mirrors reflect back everything negative, keeping it away from you.

Whenever you feel negative energy starting to come into your space, you can very quickly remind yourself of these mirrors, and, believe me when I say this, you will see a major difference in how other people make you feel.

Here are some affirmations for protection which you may find helpful to introduce to your day-to-day life...

- ☐ 'I only welcome and accept the most positive energies around me and in my space.'
- ☐ 'The universe is protecting me, my home and those I love.'
- ☐ 'I deserve to feel protected and I deserve to feel safe.'
- ☐ 'I am secure and safe in my life, in myself and in my surroundings.'

☐ 'I know spirit/angels/God/my loved ones [whichever you wish] is/are protecting me and is/are keeping me safe from harm.'

Some people like to use crystals for protection, and if this is the case for you, I would recommend carrying amethyst with you. Amethyst is known to protect against psychic attacks and hateful and negative energy by transmuting that energy into love, and can protect you from all types of harm and ill-wishes from others. The same is true for obsidian, black tourmaline, haematite and smoky quartz. (*More information on crystals can be found in the following chapter.*)

# 6

# CONNECTING WITH THE ENERGY AND POWER OF CRYSTALS

With stress, anxiety and depression being things so many of us face in our lives, many of us look for healing, and often for something that can help us without the need for discussing our emotional traumas and pains with others. This is why some of us turn to the energy and power of crystals. Of course, you can always turn to a spiritual advisor or therapist instead, if this is what you desire!

As interest in the spiritual and psychic has grown, so has interest in crystals. Influencers and celebrities have shared their experiences of them and the benefits of using them in their day-to-day lives. Adele explained to the *Sun* how crystals helped her manage stage fright, for example, while Kim Kardashian has mentioned how crystals inspired her to create her perfume bottle (reported by US magazine.com).

Although crystals are very pretty, sometimes enchanting, and can capture the imagination, they aren't just that. Most crystals form naturally as minerals within the Earth, and it is believed that these minerals carry energy – energy that is known to help us in all areas of our lives. Today, scientists use quartz crystals in watches due to their unique gravitational field. Ancient cultures were also aware of the healing power of crystals; it's believed ancient Egyptians, for example, had large crystal temples for healing.

It is very often believed that holding crystals, carrying them and placing them on the body can bring mental, emotional and physical benefits, the idea being that they connect with your own energy field, bringing you relief for a number of things such as stress, emotional pain and depression. Some believe that crystals have the power to heal physical ailments and illnesses too, although this is not scientifically proven.

Knowing how to connect with crystals and to work with them will allow you to feel and see the benefits they can bring into your life.

## How to Connect with Crystals

To make an energetic connection with a crystal:

- Hold it in your palms, close your eyes and imagine it is bringing you a bright light of pure energy.

- See that energy flowing around your body from your hands up to your head, filling your whole body from head to toe.
- If you have an intention that you wish this crystal to assist you with, hold that intention in the forefront of your mind and imagine the benefits that the crystal can bring to you and your life.
- Set that intention.
- You may start to feel sensations – you may feel hot or cold, or perhaps feel a surge of energy. Is your heart racing or do you perhaps feel a sense of calm? There is absolutely no right or wrong regarding what you experience and each of us may have a very different experience when connecting with the energy of a particular crystal. It is all about trusting what feels right to you and what you feel drawn to or connected with.

## How to Cleanse Crystals

Crystals continuously charge you with their healing qualities, as long as you keep them clean. This means cleansing them once your own psychic debris has trickled into them.

This is a form of meditation, as it keeps you in a calm and serene state and open to the universal wisdom and divine messages your soul craves.

## Natural light

Moonlight is a powerful cleanser:

- Set your stones outside on the earth on a full moon before you turn in for the night and leave them to renew their healing energy by bathing in the light of the moon.
- They can be left out until morning, so go ahead and have that cup of coffee and then go and retrieve your fully recharged crystals. The Greek goddess of the moon, Selene, will have worked her magic overnight to restore and rebalance the natural healing energy of your crystals.

## Smoke

The use of smoke as a cleanser is known as smudging, and can be performed in many situations with a variety of smudging tools, such as incense, sage or palo santo. This may not be the obvious choice for anyone who is super clumsy ... but it does work.

- The first step is to open a window, This will allow all bad vibes to be released.
- After lighting your smudging tool, blow out the flame and run your crystals through the stream of fragrant smoke.
- Cleanse yourself and your crystals one by one, allowing the smoke to carry the negative vibes away.
- Upon completion of your cleansing ritual, gently place your smudge stick in a fireproof vessel until the light is completely extinguished. Let's say it again together – completely extinguished!

## Visualization

Possibly one of the most natural ways to cleanse your crystals is to use the most powerful tool at your disposal – your mind. You may be thinking, 'Yada, yada, I've heard this before.' But it is true!

- Simply find a quiet space and slip into a meditative state, while visualizing the power of your third eye to create a bright light force surrounding your crystals.
- Imagine this light filling your crystals with pure, cleansing energy and you will actually begin to feel their energy shifting within your healing hands.

Above all, regardless of which cleansing process you choose, make your intentions known by reciting a powerful mantra

CONNECTING WITH THE ENERGY AND POWER OF CRYSTALS

during your ritual. It should be something personal, repeated silently or aloud, and will help to draw away the negative energies of your crystals and restore their inner beauty and power.

# Charging

By actively charging your crystals, you can maximize the power and energy that they hold, bringing you more benefits into your life.

Here are two methods that I personally recommend for charging your crystals.

# Sunlight

Simply place your crystals in direct sunlight, as sunlight is believed to energize crystals. However, be careful how long you leave them for, as certain crystals may fade during long periods of sun exposure.

# Moonlight

Placing crystals under the light of the moon is a popular method of charging them. This is also suitable for crystals that may be sensitive to sunlight. The gentle beam of moonlight is thought to both charge and cleanse crystals, and full moons are associated with powerful energy.

# Programming

You can harness the powers of the universe to program your gemstones with specific intentions, further activating their hidden qualities, their metaphysical properties and powers. Programming is a powerful method that works in harmony with cleansing and charging. Programming also charges crystals, only not with sun or moonlight, but with your hands and mind.

## Programming crystals

- Place the crystal you wish to program in your left (receiving) hand while hovering your right (giving) one over the top of it.
- Project your intentions into the crystal, while being aware of the unique set of qualities inherent to that type of crystal. Your mind is a powerful conduit and your hands channel universal healing light and energy.

With this knowledge, you are able to program your crystals for a deeper healing experience!

## Daily guidance

Cleansing, charging and activating or programming your crystals daily is advised. They can then be held, kept on your person (in a purse or pocket), used on a shrine or altar, or meditated with daily for protection. Or you can wear them as a pendant, necklace or bracelet, always remembering that crystals protect you from environmental pollution, electromagnetic harm and negative energy.

# Centring, Grounding and Earthing

In order to harness the healing power of crystals, it is important to both centre and ground yourself with them. Centring and grounding can balance your subtle energy bodies, while activating Higher Self-awareness.

### Centring

Centring is as simple as holding a crystal in your palms while meditating and setting your intentions. It allows you to be in the ideal vibrational state before opening to receive the energy and light of the crystal. It brings your awareness to an internal space where you feel content and self-aligned. This relaxed state fosters enhanced receptivity to psychic and intuitive abilities.

## Grounding

Grounding crystals is a practice for connecting your crystals with the Earth's energy, allowing them to release any negative energies they have accumulated and restore their balance. Crystals are known to hold on to negative energies and this is a way of neutralizing and releasing this energy.

Grounding crystals is believed to be essential for them to function optimally and support their users in various spiritual practices.

Personally, when I am grounding my crystals, I will place them directly on the earth. This could be in a field, by a tree, or anywhere that I find calming.

## Earthing

Grounding crystals is linked to 'earthing', the process of burying them in soil or compost, perhaps in a garden, so they can absorb the grounding energies emanating from Mother Earth. Consider leaving your crystals buried overnight to allow for a more profound connection with the energy of the Earth.

# The Most Popular Crystals

I want to share with you some of the best-known crystals and the benefits they can bring to you and your life.

The most popular crystals are amethyst, clear quartz and rose quartz.

# Amethyst

## What is amethyst?

Known for its variation of violet tones, amethyst is a semi-precious stone and the most valuable form of quartz. Quartz is formed in magma when gas bubbles become trapped, allowing crystals to form inside the cavities created by the gas bubbles.

Amethyst has been treasured throughout history for its beauty and alleged mystical powers. It is a powerful and protective stone with a high spiritual vibration. The serenity it brings enhances higher states of consciousness and meditation.

Amethyst crystals have been used for centuries for their metaphysical healing properties. They can be beneficial to health and well-being and people use them in many different ways for healing.

## Where is amethyst from?

Most amethyst comes from Brazil, but it can also be found in Britain, Canada, East Africa, India, Mexico, Russia, Siberia, Sri Lanka, the United States and Uruguay.

# What are the healing properties of amethyst?

Amethyst is great for stability, courage, lucid dreaming and insomnia. It can also help to relieve stress and promote a sense of calmness and peace. Amethyst can aid in overcoming addictions, as it has a sobering effect on over-indulgence and physical passions, supporting sobriety.

Amethyst can also help with:

## Pain

Amethyst is good for cleansing the blood, as it relieves physical, emotional and psychological pain or stress and blocks geopathic stress to promote healing.

## Insomnia

Amethyst aids with insomnia, as it helps to improve sleep quality and bring tranquillity. Place amethyst under your pillow or on your bedside table for a peaceful night. Sleeping with amethyst can also bring intuitive dreams.

## Cleansing the aura

Amethyst smooths away physical, mental and emotional blockages, cleansing the aura.

## Stress

Amethyst is a natural tranquillizer that will reduce stress and promote relaxation by blocking geopathic stress and negative environmental energies.

## Organization

Amethyst helps us feel less scattered, more focused and in control of our faculties.

## Decision-making

Amethyst brings in common sense, aiding in the decision-making process, and helps us put decisions and insights into practice.

## Mentally

Amethyst is calming and aids the transmission of signals in the brain, helping ease the strain of an overactive mind.

## Anxiety

As amethyst balances out highs and lows to promote emotional centring, it can help ease anxiety and bring peace of mind. It will remove feelings of anger, rage and fear, and alleviate sadness.

## Spiritually

Amethyst is a powerful spiritual crystal, as it gives insights into the true nature of the divine and encourages selflessness.

## How to cleanse amethyst

Cleansing amethyst crystals is essential to ensure that they are working to their fullest potential. You can use any of the following methods:

# Sunlight

Place your amethyst crystals in direct sunlight for a few hours - though not for longer, as amethyst can fade! Sunlight will help to clear any negativity or energy blockages.

# Moonlight

Place your amethyst crystals outside under the moon's light. The moon's energy will help to recharge and revitalize them.

# Saltwater

Soak your amethyst crystals in saltwater for a few hours. The salt will help to clear any negative energy or blockages.

### Is amethyst water safe?

Yes, amethyst is water safe, and you can also make the best crystal water to drink! (*See below for crystal water.*) Crystals help clear and cleanse water of any impurities, and the water gets infused with the crystals' healing energy. Drinking amethyst crystal water can help to improve your overall health and well-being.

## What zodiac sign is amethyst associated with?

Amethyst is associated with the zodiac sign of Pisces. It helps those born under this sign to tap into their creativity and intuition, but anyone can utilize amethyst to promote healing and relaxation, regardless of their zodiac sign.

## Which month is amethyst the birthstone for?

Amethyst is the birthstone for February.

# Clear quartz

## What is clear quartz?

Clear quartz is one of the world's most abundant and versatile crystals. It absorbs, stores, releases and regulates energy, and can be used for everything from cleansing other crystals to amplifying the energy of your personal space. It is the most powerful healing and energy amplifier on the planet because of its unique helical spiral crystalline form.

Clear quartz amplifies and strengthens the whole aura by cleansing and shifting energy. It draws off negative energy of all kinds, neutralizing background radiation, including electromagnetic smog and petrochemical emanations. It balances and revitalizes the physical, mental, emotional and spiritual planes, cleanses and enhances the physical organs and subtle bodies and acts as a deep soul cleanser, connecting the physical dimension with the mind.

It can be programmed with intentions and then used as a tool to boost those thoughts and help you manifest your dreams. It works at a vibrational level attuned to the specific energy requirements of the person needing healing or undertaking spiritual work. It takes the energy to the most perfect state possible, going back to before any disease or bad intentions set in.

There are endless possibilities when it comes to using clear quartz in your personal space. You can use it to amplify the energy of your intentions and desires. You can also use it to create a protective barrier around your space, keeping out negative energies. Whether you're using it for cleansing, protection or amplification, clear quartz is a powerful ally in creating the life you desire.

## Where is clear quartz from?

Clear quartz is formed in igneous rocks. It is created when a silicon dioxide solution crystallizes as it cools and hardens. Slow cooling typically allows the quartz crystals to grow larger. The silicon dioxide molecules arrange themselves in a hexagonal lattice, and *voilà*, clear quartz!

Clear quartz is relatively common and can be sourced worldwide.

## What are the healing properties of clear quartz?

As the 'master healer', clear quartz can be used for any purpose. No matter how you choose to use it, it is a powerful tool for amplifying energy and intention. When working with this crystal, always set your intention clearly and let the crystal do the work. Trust that the universe will provide what you need.

Clear quartz is by far the most versatile and multi-dimensional stone in the mineral kingdom as far as its healing properties are concerned. These include:

### Guidance

If you need guidance in your life, look no further. Clear quartz is a beautiful gem for providing guidance and clarity in situations we are struggling to resolve.

Ask your clear quartz a question that's on your mind. Allow its energy to guide you towards the solution and thank it for its help.

### Positivity

Clear quartz can help by radiating positivity into every corner, bringing in new life where there was once only stagnant energy.

If you're feeling negative, you can turn it around by holding the crystal in your non-dominant hand, taking a few deep breaths of awareness and asking it to help you release the negativity with simple meditation.

Through alleviating emotional pain and releasing energetic blockages, clear quartz will set you free and let light in.

## Focus

Looking for a way to clear your mind and focus on your intentions? Look no further than the power of clear quartz. This healing crystal is known for its ability to clear away negativity and help us stay focused on our goals.

It also helps to reveal the truth and brings clarity of mind, allowing us to focus on what's essential in life.

It is said to be a stone of new beginnings, so if you're looking for a fresh start or extra help manifesting your goals, consider working with clear quartz.

## Meditation

This crystal raises the vibrations of any surrounding crystals and amplifies them. It will only enhance positive energy, leaving negativity behind. Channelling specific energy into clear quartz during meditation will send it out into your space, filtering out distractions and leaving you surrounded with blissfulness.

## Spirituality

Spiritually, clear quartz raises energy to the highest possible level. This crystal also cleanses and enhances the organs and subtle bodies and acts as a deep soul cleanser, connecting the physical dimension with the mind.

Clear quartz also stores information like a natural computer; these crystals are a spiritual library waiting to be accessed.

## How to cleanse clear quartz

There are a few different ways to cleanse clear quartz.

# Sea salt

One popular method is to bury it in sea salt for 24 hours. This will remove any negative energy that it has absorbed.

# Sunlight

Another way to cleanse this crystal is to put it in direct sunlight for at least an hour. Sunlight is a natural cleanser that will help recharge and rejuvenate the crystal.

# Use it to cleanse other crystals

If you want to use clear quartz to cleanse other crystals, you can place it next to the one(s) you wish to cleanse. Its energy will help remove any negative energy from the other crystal(s).

You can also place a piece of clear quartz in your crystal collection to balance everything energetically.

## Is clear quartz water safe?

Yes, clear quartz is water safe. You can cleanse your crystals in running water or even soak them in a saltwater bath. Just be sure to dry them off afterwards, so they don't become waterlogged.

## What zodiac sign is clear quartz associated with?

This crystal is associated with the zodiac signs of Virgo and Capricorn.

## Which month is clear quartz the birthstone for?

Clear quartz is the birthstone for April.

# Rose quartz

## What is rose quartz?

Rose quartz is a beautiful pink crystal known for its incredible ability to promote love and compassion.

It is formed through the process of magma crystallization. This process begins when magma is pushed up towards the Earth's crust and makes its way through empty pockets of stone, picking up different minerals along the journey. Eventually, it rises enough to cool, meaning that the magma that entered stone pockets is trapped there while it cools. As the magma cools, silicon mixes with oxygen and begins to form quartz crystal. The crystal grows as more silicon and oxygen combine. If titanium is present during the cooling process, it will integrate with the silicon and oxygen, creating an impurity in the quartz, which brings about a rose-coloured appearance, creating rose quartz.

This powerful stone opens the heart chakra, allowing us to experience more profound levels of love and understanding in both ourselves and others.

Rose quartz is therefore perfect for gifting to a loved one to express your love and help guide them to a higher level of affection. If you're looking for a beautiful anniversary, birthday or Valentine's gift, look no further.

## Where is rose quartz from?

Rose quartz is found worldwide, but it's believed to have originated in eastern Brazil. Additionally, it can be sourced from South Africa, the United States, Japan, India and Madagascar. Today, this crystal is found in many different settings, from mines and quarries to rivers and streams.

## What are the healing properties of rose quartz?

This gemstone promotes a wide range of mental, emotional and physical benefits. Some of the key healing properties of rose quartz include:

### Calming and soothing

Rose quartz has a gentle, calming energy that can help soothe feelings of stress, anxiety and anger, making it suitable for use in cases of trauma or crisis.

## Emotionally
Rose quartz releases unexpressed emotions and heartache; it soothes internalized pain and heals deprivation.

## Promoting love
Rose quartz is known for its ability to promote love and compassion in ourselves and others. It teaches us how to love ourselves, which is vital if we have judged ourselves and thought ourselves unlovable. Loving yourself is crucial for accepting love and giving love to others. In the wise words of RuPaul, 'If you can't love yourself, how the hell you gonna love somebody else?'

Rose quartz will also encourage self-forgiveness and acceptance, invoking self-trust and self-worth. Placing a rose quartz by your bed will help attract love and relationships to you. Rose quartz is also decisive for promoting love in existing relationships by restoring trust and harmony to encourage unconditional love.

## Negativity
Rose quartz gently draws off negative energy and replaces it with loving vibes. Therefore, if you're looking to strengthen empathy and sensitivity to aid the acceptance of necessary change, consider getting some rose quartz.

*Spirituality*

Rose quartz can also be beneficial for those seeking to align more closely with their spiritual path, as it helps to open the heart chakra and allows us to connect more deeply with our intuition and higher wisdom.

## How to cleanse rose quartz

# Sea salt or water, sage or incense

To cleanse rose quartz crystals, place them in a bowl of sea salt or water with sage leaves or incense. You can leave your crystals in the bowl overnight.

# Moonlight

You may choose to also leave the rose quartz under the moonlight if you feel the need to release and let go of any negative energy.

## Is rose quartz water safe?

Yes, rose quartz is water safe. Why not indulge in a therapeutic healing bath by placing rose quartz in your tub? Enjoy!

### What zodiac sign is rose quartz associated with?

Rose quartz is associated with the zodiac sign of Taurus, as this is a loving and nurturing stone that helps to promote stability and comfort. Virgo, Pisces and Cancer can also benefit from it. It should be noted, though, that anyone can use rose quartz to promote healing, regardless of their zodiac sign.

### Which month is rose quartz the birthstone for?

Rose quartz is the birthstone for January.

Now let's delve into some of the crystals that are not so common or well known but may be beneficial to you when developing your psychic abilities!

## Crystals Recommended for Psychic Development

### Angelite

Angelite is ideal for mediumship and channelling, as it increases inner guidance, converts fear into faith and promotes psychic abilities such as astral travel. It is beneficial for creative and psychic people, due to its link to the higher realms. It sparks inner peace, conscious awareness, tranquillity, angelic contact and psychic healing powers! It enhances telepathy between you and your clients, or you and the people in your personal life. It is great for spiritual journeys within (inside) and without (externally).

Universal truths become known with angelite. It's a powerful stone for healers, spiritual teachers and practitioners of any psychic or therapeutic art. It can attune you to universal energy, heighten perception, offer protection, enhance communication and guide you to faith, universal love and benevolence. If you're struggling with forgiveness, angelite will be your faithful companion. Anxieties, fears, anger and guilt, shame and blame can be overcome with the help of this crystal.

Wholeness, healing and inner harmony are available with angelite, as is moving beyond trauma, pain and deep wounds. This miraculous gemstone facilitates the rebirthing process linked to personal alchemy, awakening and personal transformation. Psychic channelling is parked. Compassion, empathy, sensitivity, inspiration, universal knowledge, self-healing are enhanced, and divine light is allowed in.

## Aquamarine

Aquamarine is a beautiful and calming yet stimulating and soul-sparking crystal. Its blue-green colour symbolizes tranquillity, subtle perception, prophecy, clear thinking, emotional balance and intelligence, and empathy.

Aquamarine is known as 'the stone of prophets', so it is essential for your psychic development path! This beautiful, serene and Higher Self-energizing gemstone embodies the frequency of the sea and encourages positive change, movement and open-mindedness.

Creative energies also flow in abundance with aquamarine. It aids angelic and artistic communication at advanced levels, and increases well-being and positivity. It's excellent for combatting depression, isolation and irrational or illusory fears and insecurities.

Aquamarine aligns you with your life's purpose and soul mission. It's amazing for self-expression, love, friendship, business partnerships and artistic visions, and has purifying, clearing, cleansing, purging and harmonizing qualities.

## Black tourmaline

Black tourmaline is a black, opaque or slightly translucent gemstone with the powers of realignment, soul cleansing and grounding. It brings strength and stability, physical changes, and purity to your intentions.

It also protects you from harmful and negative energy, and cleanses your aura. It deflects negative energy away from you so you can find your sense of home and belonging within; clearing away karmic stories and toxic cycles provides space for the new to emerge. I personally keep a piece of black tourmaline in my bedroom, close to the windows, as it is known to repel negative energy and put psychic protection in place.

## Celestite

Celestite is a clear or sky-blue transparent crystal with a connection to the subtle, ethereal and spiritual realms. It is known as the stone of connecting with angels, and it's one of my favourites. It brings calmness, joy, serenity and harmony to all the subtle energy bodies, as well as a divine connection. It alleviates stress, anxiety, hurt, sadness and depression and enhances intuition, Higher Self alignment and contact with cosmic consciousness and the inspirational realms.

Celestite is excellent for intuition, psychic development and amplifying communication on multiple dimensions. For example, it can help you communicate better with friends, family, and business or romantic partners. It can enhance healthy and positive self-talk. It can increase communication with the divine, the imaginative realms and the Great Spirit, as well as the astral and dream realms, where great wisdom, insight and knowledge are available.

The energy of celestite is dreamy, clearing, cleansing, contemplative and meditative. Use it to connect to the unseen realms of spirit and allow visions, prophecy and help from your spirit guides to come through.

## Haematite

Haematite is an amazingly grounding gemstone that's viewed as the sacred essence of Mother Earth herself. It strengthens the physical body, blood and circulatory system by stabilizing, cleansing, clearing, aligning and providing a solid and dependable energy. It can help us be more practical, wise, discerning, logical, empathic and down to earth.

Being so grounding, haematite helps with feelings of 'being away with the fairies'. This is a great stone because it connects us to a higher spiritual power and wisdom while letting us access our practical side. It's a stone for mind, body and spirit!

Subtle, psychic and spiritual energy all increase in haematite's unique energy field. It has a strengthening, harmonizing, balancing, grounding and stabilizing effect when held, used for protection or meditation, or worked with in other ways.

Haematite's healing powers include bringing a feeling of belonging, feeling comfortable in your body and physical environment, and enjoying the prospect of limitless potential, with new beginnings, raw and unlimited creative life-force and passion too.

## Lapis lazuli

Lapis lazuli is a crystal that was revered by the ancient Egyptians. It represents inner truth, power, purification, intuition, positive magic, self-confidence and manifesta-tion. It aids friendships, protects you from negativity and psychic attack, and amplifies self-esteem and confidence.

Lapis lazuli is a powerful dream stone too, so you can use it to connect with the subtle and spiritual powers of the universe, in addition to receiving subconscious wisdom and guidance from your Higher Self in dreams.

Self-knowledge, ancient wisdom and knowledge of sacred and universal laws are part of this crystal's healing powers. Self-expression, honesty, empathy, morality and nobility increase when working with lapis lazuli. This is an amazing stone for higher channelling and divine contact. It allows you to live with a sense of wonder and grounding, wisdom and patience, and cosmic consciousness awareness and self-accountability simultaneously.

## Obsidian

Obsidian is a black crystal with white or grey markings, signifying protection, grounding and ancient wisdom with flashes of insight and inspiration. White is the colour of purity, intuition and faith, while grey represents sensibility, dependability and professionalism. Obsidian is found in volcanic regions all around the world and is formed from rapidly cooled lava (cool fact...).

Obsidian brings strength, courage and a sense of practi-cality and determination. It grounds, stabilizes, protects and strengthens. It can be used to release fears, fortify the spirit and heal and soothe deep wounds. Traumas can be transformed, repressed or hidden emotions brought to conscious light, and purging and cleansing occur on a deep level. Obsidian helps with deep wounds, secrets, memories pushed down to the subconscious, emotional instability or explosive tendencies and issues in the root chakra.

## Selenite

Selenite is a special crystal, due to its link with the moon. It is named after Selene, the ancient Greek goddess of the moon, and is transparent and white in colour. This crystal is great for the crown chakra, activating consciousness and Higher Self-awareness. It enhances spiritual gifts, increases our connection to subtle energy, and sparks divine contact. Many ancestors, guides and spirit animals communicate through selenite. It is catalytic, with the power to create internal shifts. It's ideal for all sorts of spiritual and mediumship work.

Selenite clears negative energy from our aura, awakens dormant soul gifts and protects us from psychic attack. It can heal and release negative energy or the harmful intentions of others. Our auric field gets a boost, upgrade and real cleansing and purification with selenite, so use it for all aspects of psychic mediumship and intuition. Additionally, selenite amplifies creativity, ancient wisdom and deeper self-awareness and spiritual insight. It's excellent for all channelling!

## Smoky quartz

Smoky quartz is a clear yellow-brown crystal connected to the root chakra, so perfect for all aspects of grounding. When we're connected to our root, we're able to feel secure in our body and physical environment. This makes us strong and grounded, and the feeling of security and self-preservation provided allows life-force energy to travel up through our spinal column to our crown chakra. So, the effect is an increase in vital life-force energy, psychic and spiritual powers, instincts, intuition and creativity.

Through healing and releasing blocks in the root, we become more self-realized in our divine gifts. As energy moves upwards to activate our higher energy centres, we're able to see from a higher perspective, have subtle and fine-tuned perception and access visionary and prophetic abilities. This is the effect of a strong and healed root chakra.

Kundalini energy awakens, which equates with a healthy libido, strong life-force energy, creative vision, psychic powers, enhanced sexuality and intuition. Longevity and self-love increase too.

So, new beginnings, pure potential and self-mastery are part of smoky quartz's healing domain. It's a crystal which amplifies the seeds of change, self-awareness and gentle feminine healing energy. It's linked to personal alchemy – making peace with and integrating our shadow so that fresh energy and perspectives arise. The more we integrate our shadow, the more we can embody our light.

## Sodalite

Sodalite is a powerful gemstone that will help to awaken psychic abilities. It is used to enhance the throat and third eye chakras, and sparks the Higher Self, intuition, depth, subtle perception and emotional intelligence. With the colours of the sea and sky – light blue and white – sodalite symbolizes inspiration, air, angelic connection, communication, self-expression, faith, intuition and white light.

Sodalite brings feelings of peace, comfort and serenity. It instils tranquillity, peace of mind and clear thinking, so we can see through illusions and reach the truth. It brings a mental energy that's both spiritual and intellectual. It is calming, balancing and clarifying, while promoting enhanced mental exchanges, communication and self-control.

Contemplation, introspection and meditation can all be enhanced with sodalite. Overall, this is an excellent gemstone for a developing psychic.

# 7

# TAROT AND ORACLE CARDS

Back when I first started to explore my psychic ability, I turned to the Tarot, and found it an incredibly useful tool for connecting more deeply with what I was feeling, and for bringing my intuition to the surface. Tarot and oracle cards are great tools for opening our mind to psychic and intuitive insights. They help us gain clarity on a specific area or our entire life and can bring us guidance on matters such as love, career, home and family, and even help us with past situations and guide us to our future.

## What's the Difference between Tarot Cards and Oracle Cards?

The majority of Tarot decks have 78 cards and a traditional structure. Tarot cards normally bring insight that is honest, direct and straight to the point. They do require a certain amount of learning to be able to understand the meanings of each card and how to interpret them within a reading.

I have always found cards with visual images, like the Tarot, very helpful, as I am more of a visual person. You may find through working with Tarot or oracle cards that your preference is different. But there is a wide variety of cards available and some are more visual than others.

Tarot cards are divided into two groups, the Major Arcana and the Minor Arcana. The Major Arcana (22 cards) are cards with major themes, such as The Sun, The Moon and The Lovers, whereas the Minor Arcana (56 cards) are divided into four suits, normally presented as Cups, Wands, Swords and Pentacles – the Ace of Cups, Ace of Wands, and so on. The Major Arcana are about life's big questions and themes, the Minor Arcana are about the smaller details!

On the other hand, oracle cards are normally created to bring us lighthearted insight and a general message, perhaps about what is happening that day, or the energies of the week or month ahead. You can also find oracle cards focused on angel messages, messages from heaven and so on.

Oracle cards may initially be easier to understand, as they normally come with clear messages, words or insights, either written on the cards themselves or in an accompanying booklet.

# The Tarot

The first Tarot deck I ever used was the Rider-Waite. The design of these cards goes back to the early 1900s. This is the most famous Tarot deck, and if you are looking to learn traditional Tarot, then I would definitely recommend this deck as a starting-point. I would also recommend learning the meanings of the cards in the way in which you learn best; personally, I found it easiest to connect with and learn the cards by breaking them down into sections, and I started with the major cards, the Major Arcana, the ones numbered from 1 to 22, normally in Roman numerical format.

I want to share these 22 cards with you here and help you to understand their meanings and symbology, as this will hopefully give you a kick-start in learning the Tarot. The symbology used within the Tarot is often carried throughout the cards, and you may also find this helpful when learning all the card meanings and the messages they bring us.

But first let's look at the suits of the Tarot: the Wands, Swords, Pentacles and Cups.

## The four suits - elemental energy

If you wish to start working with psychic and spiritual energy, either for yourself, your friends and family or as a business practice, you should definitely be aware of the meaning of the four suits of the Tarot. Each is linked to an element, which is also referred to as elemental energy.

## Wands

The suit of Wands is associated with Fire, primal energy, inspiration and creativity. It brings the vibrations of strength, devotion, purpose, passion, intuition and ambition. Fire energy is expansive, sparking original thought and potent life-force! So, Wands connect us to the infinite source of our pure potential, including inner creativity, imagination and soul zest. When they appear in a reading, it's a clear sign that there is a lot of power available for creation in accordance with the spiritual powers of the universe... Use it wisely.

Wands allow us to initiate projects and plant seeds that can lead to future abundance and happiness. The energy is positive, upbeat and enthusiastic – new ideas, possibilities and talents are shining through. Determination, perseverance and mental tenacity are there too. Wands can show pure creative life-force leading to the most miraculous and magical beginnings – or to disaster, chaos and destruction. This is the element of Fire at its best and worst. Fire can be hot, impulsive, quick-tempered, angry, aggressive and arrogant. It can be wild, unpredictable and over-zealous... These are the negative traits of the Wands suit.

Sexual life-force, amazing creative gifts, masculine will and strength, and the conscious mind are also represented by the Wands cards.

On a mental level, Wands symbolize higher consciousness or cosmic consciousness linked to the conscious mind. This is the part of us that is self-aware, an active participant in life.

Fire is active and direct. So, Wands represent either a positive (light) or negative (dark/shadow) manifestation of the ego. Personal energy, personality, identity and purpose come into the remit of the Wands cards.

Astrologically, this suit links to the Fire signs: Aries, Leo and Sagittarius.

When a Tarot reading is mostly Wands, we're being asked to be more charismatic, warm and friendly, as well as charming, spiritual, open-minded, creative, excited about life and its possibilities, and self-starting. Tap into the infinite source of creativity when you see Wands, while embracing your inspirational side. Also, seek greater meaning, while trying to stay clear of the egotistical and self-serving aspects of the Fire element.

## Swords

The next suit is Swords, the suit of the Air element. This suit represents the intellect, mind, thoughts, ideas, higher truths, attitudes and beliefs. It symbolizes rational, analytical and logical thought as well as imagination and intuition. Air is linked to the angelic realm, so these cards speak of higher inspirational and ethereal values and concepts.

The level of consciousness available is mental. This suit mirrors the qualities of the higher mind (positive) or lower mind (negative). These Swords are double-edged: the mind's power used for good and the mind's power used for evil. This is essentially the Higher Self/mind and Lower Self/mind division.

Air relates to movement, change and adaptability. It works in the unseen, in the invisible realms of spirit and the Ether, as well as with higher angelic or celestial forces. Air is refreshing, revitalizing and cleansing, also purging and clearing (past pains, negative karma, and so forth). It is a masculine energy connected to force, will and power. Action, ambition, courage, constructive criticism, judgement, common sense, observation, subtle perception and communication are all linked to Swords. But so are the shadow attributes of guilt, shame, a lack of compassion, the abuse of power, conflict, oppression and verbal or mental abuse.

Astrologically, Swords represent the Air signs: Gemini, Libra and Aquarius.

Seeing lots of Swords in a reading suggests we should be more thoughtful, rational, witty, intelligent and intuitive. Also, that we should start to tune into our higher mind, where limitless possibilities are achievable. Manifestation gifts are linked to Swords too.

Seeing lots of Swords can mean either confrontation and conflict are coming or communicative, intellectual and imaginative powers are soaring. As you can see from the symbol itself, swords are used to either break through things, cutting through negativity, illusions and distractions,

TAROT AND ORACLE CARDS

or cause harm through offence and attack (or defence). Mental struggles, conflict or even violence are possibilities when this suit appears, but so are angelic messages, higher inspiration and finding your purpose and life path.

## Pentacles

The suit of Pentacles relates to the element of Earth, which is dependable, grounding and practical, so Pentacles symbolize health, finances and career or legacy. There is creative energy present, and it's structured, organized and orderly. Furthermore, it's reliable, responsible and practical – we can create in a grounded and methodological way when Pentacles show up in a reading. The Earth energy is asking us to be more focused and disciplined. It is guiding us to shine our brightest light through slowing down, becoming more centred and embodying the qualities of patience, discernment and perseverance. It is determined, ambitious, level-headed, instinctive and supporting.

Pentacles lovingly guide us back to our roots, back to the core of our being. (I know this because I am an Earth sign!) They are humble, modest and completely down to earth – this is where the expression actually comes from.

External levels of consciousness, coupled with environmental clues from the physical world, come into this suit. When it appears, we are being given the chance to discover our strengths, weaknesses, likes, dislikes, unique talents, power and destiny.

Attitudes to health, finances and work are also symbolized by Pentacles. They allow us to shape, influence, create, manifest and transform directly with the universe. The energy is ordered and structured, but also innovative and inventive.

The Earth is feminine, so feminine energy is linked to Pentacles, sparking nurturing, caring, compassion, sensitivity, self-awareness and mindfulness on a deeper level. They ask us to be more grounded, decisive and responsible in all of our dealings – how we come across to others, our motivations for doing things, why we choose certain pathways or outcomes, and so forth.

The element of Earth makes us highly trustworthy; committed, loyal and faithful to friends, partners and family. It helps us grow, while simultaneously amplifying our self-esteem, personal charisma and self-worth. It helps us to be ambitious too, highly tenacious and high-achieving, while staying modest.

Finding lots of Pentacles in a reading is a call to deeper self-intimacy, ambition, resourcefulness, order, sacredness, tenacity and determination. Pentacles cards offer support, protection and fertility – they are a great sign our projects are getting a level-up or are about to generate prosperity! The abundance, self-knowledge, ancient wisdom and natural beauty of the Earth element will help as well.

Astrologically, Pentacles are symbolic of the Earth signs: Taurus, Virgo and Capricorn.

When Pentacles appear, the material aspects of life are being highlighted – a light is being shone on everything relating to the physical realm of the senses, including our physical bodies and Mother Earth.

Adopt a realistic, down-to-earth approach to life when Pentacles appear. Negative shadowy attributes to watch out for include pessimism, greed, excess materialism, rigid or inflexible mindsets. We may find ourselves over-indulging, not exercising or eating right, being overly conservative or ambitious and having too much work and no play. Generosity, kindness, selflessness, grounded vision, skilled artistry, practicality and respect for details are the positive qualities that counterbalance these aspects.

## Cups

The suit of Cups is associated with the element of Water, so relates to our emotions, feelings, instincts, internal world, subtle sensations and subconscious mind. Water is symbolic of sacredness, the imagination, the spiritual, ethereal, astral, divine and dream worlds. Cups appear in a reading when we need to tap into these areas.

The Cups suit is also concerned with relationships, love, feelings, friendships, business partnerships, family bonds and our personal connection with the universe.

Water is vast and expansive. It's linked to the unknown, as well as everything unseen and invisible. It's fluid, gentle, soft and intuitive, but powerful and healing too. It cleanses, harmonizes and balances. It reflects the sacred essence of life and self, including how connected we are to our past and future lives and soulmates, and knowledge of karmic laws and contracts. The mystical powers of the universe are seen in the Water element, so, Cups represent all of these things!

Astrologically, Cups represent the Water signs: Cancer, Scorpio and Pisces.

They also symbolize feminine energy, emotional intelligence, depth, sensitivity, divine inspiration, ancient and sacred wisdom, universal laws, knowledge of time cycles and purification. They are a direct link to the infinite, where spiritual powers, extra-sensory abilities, powerful revelations and genius imagination and creativity are available.

When we see lots of Cups in a reading, we are being asked to feel instead of think, to get in tune with our emotions and to lose the need to analyse or rationalize. Cups are about our instincts, those gut feelings and inner world sensations that lead us to self-realization and to our best creations. Creativity, romance, fantasy, seeing through illusions and nurturing psychic abilities are also connected to Cups.

Water linked to Cups represents infinity, the unlimited possibilities and potential of the human psyche and soul. It is infinite, eternal and soul-aligned, so lots of Cups in a reading portrays our need for depth and sensitivity.

Head over heart is the message here; we are being guided to trust our gut feelings and internal responses. Cups may ask us to reflect, contemplate or do some soul-searching and open ourselves up to the spiritual universe. There's a subtle and invisible energy permeating all things; Water connects us to this, and to the supernatural and super-human gifts available to us through it.

Shadowy aspects to watch out for here include being hyper-emotional, super-sensitive, apathetic, unrealistic, impractical, ungrounded and repressed. Emotions can be repressed due to feeling things way too intensely – Water is deep! This stimulates fears, wounds and trauma. Also, being disengaged, aloof and prone to fairytale love or illusions and fantasies – the negative type – is possible. Getting lost in the realm of feelings and emotions can actually lead to a lack of passion, zest and creative life-force too.

Positively, Cups represent our ability to be selfless, love unconditionally and nurture positive relationships. Family, childbirth, new projects, self-mastery, spiritual illumination and maturity and self-evolution come into their domain. And possessing high morals, ethics and integrity, due to operating on an evolved emotional and spiritual frequency...

## The Major Arcana

Now I will introduce you to the 22 cards of the Major Arcana.

## 0: The Fool

You will first notice the image of a young man standing on the edge of a cliff, as he sets out on a new adventure. He is looking up to the sky. You will notice on his shoulder he has a sack, and he has a white rose in his hand. The white rose symbolizes purity and innocence.

There is also a dog in the picture and, as we know, the dog is a loyal animal.

The Fool is looking forward, looking to the future, not the past. He is ready for a new adventure, a new beginning, a fresh start.

Just like the man in the picture, The Fool is a card of new beginnings, opportunities and potential. When you draw it, either for yourself or someone else, then you (or the person you are doing a reading for) are just at the start of a new journey, just about to start something new. You may not know where you are going and what lies ahead, but you are taking a risk, and sometimes taking a risk and stepping into the unknown is the best thing you can do.

The Fool encourages you to have an open mind, and throw caution to the wind, be open to the unknown. It reminds you that the world is your oyster and you can achieve whatever you put your mind to.

The Fool also guides you to stop holding yourself back and to step out of your comfort zone. This could be the best thing you could ever do.

## I: The Magician

The Magician is card number one, and number one in numerology, as you'll recall, is the number of new beginnings and new phases in our lives. As you'll see, on the card the Magician is dressed in a white robe, and this is a symbol of purity and protection. He also has one hand pointing up to the universe and the other pointing down to the Earth.

The Magician brings you the energy to create the life you want and make your dreams come true. When this card appears, it is time for you to move forward with creating the life you want. It is a sign for you to believe in yourself, stop procrastinating and be clear about what you want and why you want it. This is the moment to set goals, take action and focus on bringing your goals to fruition. Focus on *one* thing that will move you towards your goals and take it from there.

## II: The High Priestess

The High Priestess sits in front of two pillars, which symbolize the masculine and feminine. They also symbolize darkness and light. As you can see, the High Priestess is wearing a blue robe, blue being the colour of communication, and she has a cross around her neck, symbolizing the divine and protection. The moon at her feet symbolizes her connection with the divine feminine and intuition.

THE HIGH PRIESTESS

The High Priestess symbolizes spiritual enlightenment and divine knowledge. When this card shows up in a reading, it is showing that the veil between you and the otherworld is thin. This is a time to be still and listen to your intuition and your feelings. Your intuitive sense is guiding you to become more in touch with your own psychic awareness.

You are also being called to embrace the divine feminine, your own connection to your intuition.

## III: The Empress

The Empress is a woman with blonde hair, wearing a crown of 12 stars. You may notice the pomegranates on her robe, and pomegranates are a symbol of fertility that is associated with Aphrodite, the Greek goddess of love, so The Empress card can signify childbirth, marriage and love. There is a beautiful forest surrounding the figure of the Empress, signifying growth and grounding, and the water around her is a symbol of balance and rejuvenation. The green forest also a symbol of heart healing.

As well as being a card of healing, The Empress signifies a strong connection with femininity. It also signifies abundance, being surrounded by life's pleasures and having everything you need to live contently. When it shows up for you, you are in a period of growth and transformation and everything you have dreamed of is or very soon will be coming to fruition. It's time to connect with nature and the Earth too.

## IV: The Emperor

The Emperor is the father figure card of the Tarot. The Emperor himself sits upon a throne wearing a red robe, red being the colour of passion, but he also wears a suit of armour, showing that he is protected from any negativity that may come his way. The small river shown on the card signifies hope, letting go of negativity and bringing balance to life. The Emperor is a very protective image and is going to show up if perhaps you're feeling vulnerable or dealing with an emotional situation and need protecting from negativity or harm.

With The Emperor card bringing a fatherly presence, it can signify that you are having to be a father figure to someone right now or perhaps having to be authoritative or defensive in a situation or a specific area of your life.

The Emperor also shows that you may be taking on some kind of authority or status. You will be recognized for your efforts and hard work and commended for everything you have accomplished so far in your life.

## V: The Hierophant

The Hierophant is paired with the High Priestess, as her male counterpart. A hierophant is a religious figure, a teacher, and you'll notice that in the image, this one is sitting in front of two pillars, similar to the pillars between which the High Priestess sits. You'll notice that in his left

hand he holds a cross. This
signifies his religion, but, as we
also know, the cross is a symbol
of protection. In front of him
are two men, who are following
his wisdom and knowledge.

When this card appears in a
reading, it is time for you to
listen and learn. Perhaps it is
time to start a new course of
study, or just acknowledge how
far you have come and the things
you have learned. Perhaps it's time to put them into practice and share your knowledge and wisdom with those who
may learn and benefit from it.

The Hierophant also suggests that you may be following
the crowd and it is time to step out of your comfort zone.
You may not be willing to go into a new venture because
you are afraid, or worried about what people may think of
you. However, for your life to move forward in the way that
you want, sometimes you need to take a step out of your
comfort zone and take a risk.

## VI: The Lovers

You will notice that The Lovers card shows a male and
female, who are naked, standing in front of an angel, who is
the Archangel Raphael, the angel of healing.

The man and woman are standing in front of a pretty landscape. You can see an apple tree, which may remind you of the Garden of Eden. You may also notice the flames behind the man. Flames are a symbol of passion.

THE LOVERS

In its simplest interpretation, The Lovers card points to relationships. When this card appears within a reading, it signifies that there is a soul connection with someone significant. You may be reading for a client who is wondering if their flame is a significant one and if they are their soulmate or life partner. The Lovers does normally show a connection that is genuine, with mutual respect, compassion, acceptance and understanding of and for one another. However, be aware of the cards that come with or surround this one, as they may have a negative or positive effect on the relationship.

The Lovers card also guides you to be clear about what it is that you want in your life and what you want to work towards. What do you want to achieve and what do you truly desire? You have the choice of who you want to be in this lifetime as well as what you focus on and what you do with your time and energy. You need to be clear about what you want in order to be focused and motivated enough to achieve it.

## VII: The Chariot

The Chariot card shows a warrior who is strong and brave, driving a chariot. You may notice that he wears armour, and, as we know, this is a symbol of protection. You may also see the moons on his tunic, the moon being a symbol of 'what is coming into reality'. The thing that always strikes me about this card is that the man isn't holding

the reins of the two sphinxes pulling the chariot, and this signifies that he has faith in the universe and the divine.

You may also notice that the sphinxes are pulling in opposite directions, but the warrior remains looking forward as he steers them in a forward direction. This symbolizes that you have the determination to steer your chariot in the direction you want.

The Chariot generally indicates strength, power and determination. Maybe it has appeared because you have lost one of those recently. But this card is an encouraging one, reminding you that you can achieve whatever you put your mind to, if you keep your eyes and mind focused on the outcome and don't become distracted.

The Chariot also guides you to be assertive and to stand up for what you believe in. It shows that you have the strength to face whatever you need to and deal with whatever lies ahead of you.

## VIII: Strength

As you'll see, on the Strength card, a woman is stroking a lion on the forehead. In real life, you probably wouldn't be able to do this without the lion attacking you. In the image, its mouth is open and its teeth are showing, but it is tame. Lions aren't often tame, and this shows that either the lion is responding to the woman's energy or it is one that isn't controlling or forceful.

In *The Wizard of Oz*, the Cowardly Lion believes that his fear makes him incompetent and unable to fight or defend himself, but really he is brave and faces danger head on. So, this card shows that raw emotion, desires and will can be expressed in a positive way, without causing chaos or destruction. Your feelings are valid! In fact, they're important, and the universe wants you to express them. Subtly. Subtle control is the name of the game.

So this card is showing you that your key to success is to be both assertive and sensitive, balancing your masculine and feminine attributes.

Remember that your instincts are there to guide and serve you, not to encourage you to wage war on others or bring out their inner beasts. Your primal nature should be harmonized with your Higher Self.

The secondary symbolism here is that the woman's white robe signifies purity and innocence, as well as infinite wisdom, power and potential (the infinity symbol lies on top of her head). Commitment and sheer devotion are available to you when this card appears.

The Strength card also indicates that you are pushing yourself forward in life with your own strength, determination and perseverance. You have the confidence to overcome the obstacles that are in front of you or may come your way. The fears, challenges and doubts could even be mostly in your mind or made to appear worse by overthinking or catastrophizing.

## IX: The Hermit

The Hermit stands on top of a mountain, high above what is below him. He holds a lantern with a star alight in it, the six-pointed star being a symbol of wisdom and knowledge. The lantern lights the path ahead, but only the immediate path – the Hermit can only see so far.

167

The Hermit is reminding you that everything is revealed to us when it is meant to be, and that sometimes things appear gradually as we move into the future, and some of those things may not be fully revealed to us at this time.

The Hermit may show that you need to take a break from the 'norm' right now and focus on what satisfies your needs, both mentally and emotionally. He is inviting you to retreat from the outside world whenever you need to, to ignore distractions and withdraw from those who may be troubling you.

You may be taking part of your journey alone at this time, or you may feel alone, but that is OK – The Hermit card also shows that within your heart you hold all the answers that you need, and all you have to do is listen to your intuition.

## X: The Wheel of Fortune

The Wheel of Fortune represents good luck, positive karma
and breaking negative cycles. It
is depicted as a giant wheel, with
a snake, the Egyptian god
Typhon, the god of evil, Anubis,
the Egyptian god of the dead,
and a sphinx, a symbol of
ancient knowledge and strength.
There are also four winged creatures representing the zodiac

WHEEL OF FORTUNE

signs of Aquarius (the angel), Scorpio (the eagle), Leo (the lion) and Taurus (the bull).

The Wheel of Fortune reminds you that life is in a constant state of change and movement. Energies shift and luck comes and goes due to past actions and intentions. The seeds we plant can reap positive or negative karma. The Wheel of Fortune represents a change of fate, fortune turning in your favour. Cherish the blissful and happy moments while they last, because you never know when your luck might change.

If you're down on your luck right now, the Wheel of Fortune appears to tell you that your destiny involves ups and downs, highs and lows. Have patience. What goes around comes around. What you send out to the universe will come back to you in time...

## XI: Justice

The Justice card is about fairness, truth and karma, and it can be a reference to the law. The figure on the card, as you will see, holds a sword in her right hand. A sword is a weapon of the intellect, which can point to someone's actions, either good or bad.

If you draw Justice, you are being guided to look at your

behaviours and actions and remember that choices have consequences. If there is any reason for you to make a decision and Justice turns up in a reading, then you may be involved in a legal case or hearing from someone from a professional body. When the Justice card appears, I intuitively feel that you have nothing to worry about if you have acted with the best intentions; however, if there has been some sneaky behaviour, then it will definitely come to light.

## XII: The Hanged Man

Surrender, letting go, embracing new perspectives and being suspended in time are the meanings of The Hanged Man. The man's face is calm and serene, showing he has accepted his current stagnation. Divine or perfect timing is the main message; everything happens with perfect timing, and now you must wait. Your destiny is being put on hold.

The man has a halo around his head, which signifies purity and innocence. Insight, self-awareness, higher wisdom, spiritual perspectives and enlightenment are part of the Hanged Man's meaning. One of his feet is bound to the tree, while the other is free, representing your capacity to free yourself from limitations or restrictions in due course.

Stagnation is only temporary. The man's blue vest symbolizes knowledge, so you already have all the wisdom you need to break through. His pants are red, symbolizing passion, vitality and the physical body. Ultimate surrender coupled with martyrdom and sacrifice are necessary right now for the greater good, or for your soul mission and spiritual path.

You are being asked to put things on hold and await the next step, while releasing old and outdated belief systems and patterns of behaviour. With patience and trust in the divine plan, you will see new opportunities coming your way. Meanwhile, you have time to pause, evaluate and contemplate.

## XIII: Death

Endings, change, transformation, transition, purging and cleansing on a soul level are the meanings of the Death card. This is positive, as releasing the old leads to new space and opportunities. Fresh energy will be coming once old chapters and parts of yourself 'die'.

The card itself shows a skeleton dressed in black armour, riding a white horse. Death holds a five-petalled rose, symbolizing beauty, compassion and serenity, as well as purification and immortality. This shows that there is positivity and joy to be found in the hard times. All endings lead to beginnings – transitions are necessary for your soul's evolution.

The death of the ego, physical loss, a job or health ending, or 'death' in any area of life are associated with this Tarot card. The message is that you must let go of the outworn and embrace essential endings. You can't be clinging on to old cycles. Major transformation is in order, so be open to new beginnings.

Take heart, for while painful chapters are ending, new doors are opening. There is a cleansing and purging occurring that can lead to awakening, abundance and eternal satisfaction.

## XIV: Temperance

Balance, moderation, patience, purpose and alignment are symbolized by the Temperance card. This is the ultimate realignment and self-healing card, sparking inner stability and recovery from stressful or chaotic situations.

It features a large winged angel with both masculine and feminine attributes. She wears a light blue robe, signifying wisdom, inspiration and imagination, with the symbol of a triangle inside a square. This symbol portrays human consciousness being bound to the Earth, to the material realm. The angel has one foot in water and the other on rocks, and stands balanced between the two, which suggests the need for balance in your life.

In the background there's a path winding up a mountain, a symbol of prestige, achievement and enlightenment or victory. A golden crown hovers above the mountain. The message is to take the higher path, restore order with grace, morality and dignity, and regain your flow, listen to your heart and trust your intuition. Your crown chakra needs to be awakened and activated for all of your material pursuits to come to fruition. Remain calm, keep a check on your emotions and stay composed, even in the most stressful of situations. Respect for balance, tranquillity and patience will see you through anything. In terms of work, Temperance represents cooperation, teamwork, solidarity in diversity and harmony.

## XV: The Devil

Attachment, addiction, restriction, oppression and the shadow self are shown by The Devil card. One of the less positive Tarot cards, it represents oppression and the forces of will. A Satanic figure is depicted binding two people together with chains, with a strong emphasis on sexuality. Sexuality can be part of the shadow self, as it's something we tend to deny, reject or repress.

THE DEVIL

If this card has appeared for you, you are currently being oppressed or restricted, but you have the wisdom to see you through. You might be bound to ideas, a relationship, people, places or environments which aren't good for your soul. You're being suppressed and limited, and it's taking a toll on your health and finances! You need to break free, and to do so, you must accept that you do have control.

The Devil card is about taking accountability and responsibility, and not playing the victim. Yes, there are external forces restricting you, yet you also have the power to take back control of yourself. Self-mastery is on the horizon, but first you must be totally honest about your feelings, actions or inactions, and emotions.

You can break free of shadow traits and toxic behaviours! Negative patterns are not the final chapter of your story. Lust, animalistic desires and the primal body are key meanings of

The Devil, and these need to be healed and transcended, or, at the very least, brought into greater balance.

## XVI: The Tower

THE TOWER

People are normally afraid when they see The Tower card, as the image of a tower burning down can appear alarming, but there is no need to have any fear!

Yes, The Tower symbolizes sudden change, upheaval and chaos, but also revelation and awakening. It shows a tall tower perched on top of a rocky mountain being struck by lightning, which sets it on fire. Two people are leaping from a window.

The Tower represents chaos and destruction, and that the structures of your life are built on insecure and rocky foundations – false premises, false promises, lies, manipulation and faulty belief systems. This card's message is one of faulty and unstable foundations coming crashing down. This could mean a divorce, death, a major ending in career, health or family, or a natural disaster. All things false or fake must fall. But out of their collapse comes a burst of insight, inspiration and even telepathic connection with another or a group.

Chaos and upheaval lead to new energy, fresh perspectives and brand new chapters. Universal healing and life-force energy and light flow down through your crown chakra, which stimulates awakening and transformation.

Divine intervention is the symbolism and meaning here. Change is here to shake things up and wake you from your slumber, from a dream created a long time ago. The Tower destroys all that isn't meant for your Higher Self or true path. Your highest good is supported by the universe.

Illusions are coming to an end when this card appears. Unstable structures are burning and falling, while systems more representative of reality are coming into being, and realizations leading to self-actualization are possible.

## XVII: The Star

Hope, faith, purpose and renewal are part of The Star's message. The card depicts a naked woman kneeling at a pool with two containers of water; one represents the subconscious and the other the conscious. She is a symbol of fertility, alchemizing emotions, instincts and feelings into the realm of thought, intellect and ideas.

The Star signifies a period of peace, rest, serenity, tranquillity and self-reflection. Additionally, abundance, prosperity and stardom! Your rewards are coming from good karma, pure intentions, hard work, altruism and staying faithful and committed to your life path. The Star represents success, prestige and legacy, also fame, justice and life purpose.

You're returning to your core essence, your divine and pure nature, when this card appears for you. All faulty and distorted belief systems are being stripped back.

Hope, faith, inspiration, spiritual illumination and limitless possibilities are further meanings of this card. Slow down and allow yourself to dream and journey within, as this is where you will find magic and your true north star.

## XVIII: The Moon

The Moon represents fear, anxiety, illusion, intuition and the subconscious mind. The ability to see through illusions, coupled with intuition, imagination and potent instincts, is available to you when this card appears in a reading. You may be a real BS detector or a skilled psychic, healer or Tarot reader. The Moon also represents the

YOU MUST BE PSYCHIC

divine feminine attributes within us all, which are linked to sacred law and order.

With this card, you're being asked to connect to your dreams and explore the vast landscapes of the astral, multi-dimensional and dream worlds. You're also being guided to become more conscious of the people in your waking life, as there could be some manipulation and deception present.

The actual card depicts a full moon in the night sky, positioned between two large towers. The moon's light is dim, but illuminates the path to higher consciousness, which is further highlighted through a small crayfish crawling out of the pool below, symbolizing the early stages of consciousness unfolding. A dog and a wolf are involved – symbols of the tamed and wild aspects of our minds.

Unconscious projection, shadow mirroring and circulating toxicity are integral to this card. Emotional distress or painful wounds are being brought to light. You are holding on to repressions and suppressions, pain, trauma and unhealed wounds. This is making you project your fears and insecurities and lash out at others.

But the subconscious is becoming conscious, and this is the way to heal the pain. The Moon card advises you to see a shamanic practitioner or energy worker, attend regular moon circles or healing workshops, and receive Tarot or psychic readings or sound healing sessions. Hypnosis and self-therapy can also help.

## XIX: The Sun

Positivity, warmth, success, fun and vitality, in addition to supreme optimism and empowerment are part of The Sun's symbolism. On the card, the sun is large and bright in the sky, representing the source of creation, and there's a young naked child representing joy, inner spirit, the inner child, purity and innocence, on a white horse,  signifying purity, faith, nobility, inner strength and freedom of expression.

This is a message of abundance, radiance and success, with prestige, accomplishment and inspiration of all kinds too. When this card comes to you, you are bringing warmth, beauty, love, peace and protection to others – when you let yourself experience these things, that is. It's *your* authenticity that motivates others to be themselves.

Life is good with The Sun; there is a divine flow of prosperity, happiness and health coming to you. You're powerful, authoritative and driven by a need for connection and intimacy, rather than ego satisfaction or selfish desires. You're being asked to embody these things, if you aren't already. Divine will and creative power are ready to flow through you now. Live with more passion and joy!

## XX: Judgement

The Judgement card symbolizes rebirth, inner calling, judgement and divine purpose. It depicts naked men, women and children with Archangel Gabriel, the messenger of God, blowing his trumpet in the skies. This is a symbol of hearing the call of your soul and responding to it. The extensive mountain range in the background represents the

challenges and obstacles you have had to overcome, the trials and tribulations of your past.

A higher level of consciousness is available to you now. You're experiencing a spiritual awakening and realizing you're destined for so much more than before. You're attuning to a higher frequency, your old self is being released and you're stepping into a brand-new version of yourself.

Further meanings of Judgement are a life-changing decision, a significant change, absolution, karmic completion, a unified picture of your life's story, putting together the final missing pieces and integrating deep wounds for future self-alignment. The past is behind you and you've cleared wrongdoings, regrets and guilt, as well as a lack of forgiveness. You're ready for new challenges!

## XXI: The World

The final Major Arcana card, The World, is a symbol of integration, completion, travel, accomplishment and personal closure. It shows a naked woman wrapped in a purple cloth, the colour of vision and intuition, and with her eyes glancing back at her past while her body moves forwards, towards her future.

She's holding the infinity symbol in her hands, like the Magician. There's a wreath with a lion, bull, cherub/angel and eagle, and the message is of the cyclic nature of existence. You're being guided into a new phase, the next stage of your journey. Wholeness, achievement, fulfilment, completion and things coming full circle in your life are key to The World.

There could be a gradation, birth or long-term aspiration or dream manifesting now. Your purpose and life path are in full motion – everything you've envisioned is coming to pass. Spiritual lessons have been fully integrated, while the shadow setbacks that once kept you blocked or stagnant have been balanced and transcended.

Finally, this is an invitation to reflect on your journey, celebrate your wins and energize new goals and aspirations.

If you still have loose ends, tie them up. Close old chapters, so a whole new life and world can emerge.

# Oracle Card Readings and Tarot Spreads

So, how do you carry out a Tarot or oracle card reading? Are there any common spreads?

How do you get a deck in the first place? When I went to get my first Tarot deck back in 2010, I was told that a Tarot deck had to be gifted to you, but that is a superstition, and I'd just like to clarify that you are able to purchase Tarot cards for yourself.

I would also like to say that when it comes to purchasing your first Tarot deck, go with whatever you feel drawn to or guided to. It may be that you are drawn to the images or the way the cards look or feel. Either way, trust your gut when it comes to which cards you buy. It may be that you have to try a few different decks to figure out what works best for you.

## How to do a reading

It's so important that when you come to do a reading, your mind is clear and your energy is calm. As I mentioned earlier on, it's only when your mind is clear that you are able to hear your intuitive thoughts and nudges clearly. So, you may want to carry out a quick meditation to relax and clear your mind before starting a reading.

Once your mind is clear:

> Begin by closing your eyes, centring yourself and taking some deep breaths. Personally, I take my cards in my hands and hold them over my heart, close my eyes for a moment and clarify what my intention is. Is it to receive guidance or insight for myself or for someone else? Is there a particular area of my life or their life that I would like to receive guidance on? Your gut and your intuition will always guide you to what it is that you need to know at that particular moment. That means that the most troubling issues or concerns will immediately come to the surface of your or your client's mind, and normally the focus of the reading will revolve around that.

Can you read for yourself? Yes, I believe you can receive a certain amount of guidance or general insight. It may not be as specific as what you can get intuitively for another person, but you can get some guidance on your life now, a specific area or the future through your own Tarot or oracle cards. How do you do it?

## Shuffling

There are a few ways to shuffle a card deck. Personally, I like to shuffle the cards until a card or number of cards falls out or catches my attention. Sometimes in my gut I will have a sudden nudge to stop shuffling or to pull a certain card. I trust the feelings I get. You may find the more you use your cards and connect with them, the 'louder' your feelings and nudges are when you're shuffling and drawing the cards.

## Laying out the cards

You may ask your intuition about how many cards to draw from the Tarot deck. You can draw as few as one card or as many as your space allows. You may choose to use a particular Tarot spread (*see page 185*).

- Once you have pulled your cards, lay them out in front of you, face down or face up, whichever you prefer. They can either come out 'upright' or 'reversed'. Upright cards bring the face-value message of the card, while reversed cards bring the opposite meaning: a warning, something you need to watch out for, or a positive message if the card meaning is negative.

- If you don't get a couple of immediate thoughts when looking at your cards, sit with them calmly for a minute or two and see what floats to the surface. Remember, don't overthink it – when we overthink it, not only do we block our intuition, but we stop the guidance from flowing through to us.

# The most common Tarot spreads

A Tarot spread is simply laying the cards out in such a way that there is a particular focus for each card to help you when it comes to receiving clarity in specific areas, for example love and romance, career, past, present and future.

## The three-card spread

You can use a simple three-card spread to look at your past, present and future. You may use this to see how a key influence from the past affects a current situation. You can also explore how your current outlook on life and your decisions affect your future. I would recommend a three-card spread if you are looking for a sneak peek into your life at this time.

## The Celtic Cross spread

If you are looking for a little more depth in your reading, then the Celtic Cross spread will be perfect for you, as with this Tarot spread you draw twelve cards for more insight rather than three cards for a brief outlook.

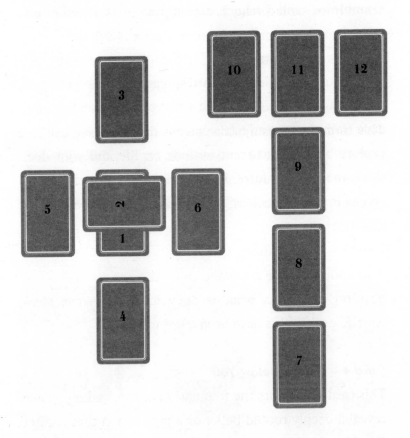

We'll break down the Celtic Cross in the same way that we do with other standard tarot spreads, by looking at the positions of the cards:

### Card 1 - The Present

Sometimes called 'the heart of the matter', this card represents your present circumstances and the energy surrounding you. It reveals the focus of the reading.

### Card 2 - What Crosses You

This card is seen as a bridge connecting the three cards of past (5), present (1), and near future (6). 'What crosses you' can represent hurdles (or people) that are preventing you from moving smoothly towards your desired goal.

### Card 3 - What's Above You

Also known as 'the crowning card', the 'what's above you' position represents what is on your mind. What ideas, worries or thoughts have been consuming you?

### Card 4 - What's Below You

This card represents the foundation of the reading. It may reveal a deeply rooted belief or a past action that created the framework for today's situation. This card may also help you to identify repeating patterns that are holding you back.

## Card 5 - The Past

Everybody has a past, but what is revealed here is relevant in terms of the journey between the past, present and future cards. See 'the past' as what has happened recently that has contributed to who you are today.

## Card 6 - The Near Future

This card represents what is going to happen next. Remember, this is not the outcome of the entire reading. See it as the next notable phase before the story is concluded with the last three cards. This card usually manifests pretty quickly, sometimes within days.

## Card 7 - Your Personality

This card reveals your personality traits or how you feel about yourself. If you draw Death, for example, it could mean you are feeling exposed or are ready to end an old way of being. The Two of Swords could indicate you are indecisive. The Empress might suggest you are feeling broody or motherly, and so on.

## Card 8 - Environment

This card describes your environment at work or home. If you find someone overbearing, such as a moody relative or a bullying boss, they may appear in this position. It depends on how much impact they have on you.

### Card 9 - Hopes and Fears
Positive cards here reflect your ambitions, and negative cards can indicate where you feel the grip of fear.

### Cards 10, 11 and 12 - The Outcome
These three cards sum up the outcome of the reading, as in what will occur in the future. As a rule of thumb, these cards usually manifest within twelve months. However, I tend to find them playing out much earlier.

## Intuitive reading (Trusting your instincts)
When getting to grips with the Tarot cards, I would often just draw one card per day. This wouldn't only help me to get an understanding of the cards without learning too much at once, but would also give me perhaps a general theme for the day or a little bit of insight into that particular time. This is the power of your subconscious mind. Your subconscious mind, in harmony with your soul and Higher Self, speaks through the cards.

To give yourself an intuitive reading:

- Close your eyes, go within for a few moments and connect to the source of light and spirit within you.
- Then ask for the card or cards that have your best interests at heart. Physical reality is an extension of your inner world, so you will pull the 'perfect' cards, the ones that are meant for you.

# 8

# MANIFESTATION AND THE LAW OF ATTRACTION

Enlightenment, finding the light within and around, is to awaken to the divine purpose of your soul. It's your soul mission, your life path and your ultimate purpose, and to truly live it, you must have knowledge of the universal laws.

## Metaphysics 101: The 12 Universal Laws

The 12 universal laws can be seen as fundamental focus points as well as a foundation for your psychic gifts. They are primary areas for insight, self-discovery and wisdom, including pathways to higher self-realization and personal awakening. They are unchanging laws that are intuitively known and felt by many, regardless of race, sex, gender, sexuality, religion, ethnicity and other separating factors.

The number of universal laws is debatable. Some say there are seven, a number associated with light and spirituality, while others suggest twelve, the number of star signs and main meridians in the body. I believe a clue lies in numerology and the patterns found in natural cycles, and therefore there are twelve, as follows:

## Divine oneness

The first law is about the interconnectedness of all things. Everything is connected on a subtle level, and you may call this 'subtlety' the subconscious, or the angelic, spiritual, astral, ethereal, higher-dimensional or multi-dimensional planes.

Subtle energy connects every living being on Earth. It also connects non-human entities, both on Planet Earth and in the cosmos. If we look at a human or animal eye, for instance, it will look like the universe, or even a specific galaxy. Every part of the physical body, as well as every thought, feeling, emotion, action and sensation, is connected to everything else.

In terms of intuitive powers, this implies that we can look to the divinity that connects us to ourselves, other humans, the planet and all sentient creatures, and both our inner world and outer world for healing and spiritual growth.

If we're feeling disconnected, disempowered or simply low and uninspired, reminding ourselves of the Law of

YOU MUST BE PSYCHIC

Divine Oneness will help us to reconnect to our true selves, and to our psychic and intuitive gifts.

Divine energy flows through all living things. We are divine creatures, and the ultimate purpose of using our gifts is to help others rediscover their divine spark. It's a beautiful gift.

## Vibration

Vibration rules everything – all life on Earth and the universe itself. The sound of creation, often said to be *Om*, is believed to be a unique and specific frequency that formed the universe. Sound and silence, being and emptiness, form and formlessness – everything exists as a vibratory frequency. This is why we have a term that sounds familiar and resonates with us – 'vibes'. We all give off vibes, just as we all receive them. Thoughts, feelings, emotions, projections and beliefs interact to create positive or negative experiences. Are we positively mirroring one another and treating everyone as a reflection of ourselves? Or are we projecting and allowing our unconscious fears and insecurities or annoyances to ripple out and meet our mirrors negatively?

It's our thoughts, emotions, and intentions that shape and create reality as we know it. We shape, create and influence the physical world through inner world sensations and perspectives, observations and conclusions. So, understanding the basic and perhaps more complex principles of vibration is crucial to your path as a psychic healer. To heal, you must first get to the root of blocks, and to find the root cause you must be aware of vibrations.

## Correspondence

This third universal law states that we're all mirrors of one another, but this doesn't just signify humans, but also relates to the way we mirror animals, plants and the universe itself. Within is without, internal is external, as above, so below. Patterns and cycles can be found in all of nature.

In terms of your special gifts, working with the various modes and channels for healing that are available to you will show you how life is cyclic. You may think you've learned a lesson, healed a pattern of thought or behaviour, or transcended something contributing to your ill-health and imbalance, but then it will re-emerge at another time. The Law of Correspondence portrays the non-linear and cyclic nature of time. Time is, in fact, an illusion.

The Law of Correspondence is very powerful when it comes to helping your clients, because you can slow down and be totally present with them. Through presence, you begin to truly perceive how past, present and future inter-act to prevent them from living their best lives. In addition to providing communication and guidance from loved ones in spirit, you can sense things below the surface.

One simple yet clear example is sensing a hidden or as yet undiscovered illness. You can use the fact that time is an illusion and non-linear to understand, with the help of your Higher Self, how someone's specific and self-sabotaging actions are contributing to something serious, or something long term. You might sense that a bad daily habit that seems completely trivial to everyone else is leading to a bigger future event, like an illness or injury. It's not about being pessimistic or using your powers to make money from a client's suffering; the intention is to be present and connect to your client's holistic self, with love, to gain a more complete view of their situation.

## Attraction

The best-known law, the Law of Attraction, shows the power of our thoughts and intentions to attract abundance and positive experiences in harmony with our Higher Self and our best lives.

Focus on what you want, and you shall receive, in short. This is the basis of this law. But there needs to be a level of self-mastery and control in order to receive what your heart desires. Is what you're seeking in alignment with your heart, the space of unconditional love, self-love and compassion, and your Higher Self and mind, the part of you that is connected to cosmic consciousness and the divine? It's not as simple as the ego wanting something. For the Law of

Attraction to work, you must connect to your heart space. Your higher mind must want it too, so you know that having it will serve your soul's purpose or life's mission in some way.

This is why focusing every day on manifesting an expensive car or winning the lottery might not produce results, yet putting your energy and attention into manifesting health, healing and recovery from addictions or limiting beliefs may just change your life. This is how the Law of Attraction works. Like attracts like, yet that 'like' must be genuinely good for you, good for your Higher Self.

In terms of your service as a psychic, the Law of Attraction can help you to manifest the resources, finances and opportunities or partnerships needed to do great work in the world. It's all very well wishing and dreaming and hoping and praying for a successful career, but there needs to be financial, practical and material aspects in place for it to happen. This universal law is perfect for creating a bridge between the spiritual and material worlds.

## Inspired action

Actionable steps and conscious action are what's needed after the Law of Attraction has done its work. It's not enough to simply think and attract, you need to take the steps towards success and achievement.

Life involves dualities and polar opposites – yin and yang, for example, passivity and action, feminine and masculine, receptivity and assertiveness. Together, they create unity, balance and wholeness. Without one of the two, there would be a missing ingredient for creation.

The Law of Inspired Action implies that to create we need to slow down, be in stillness and silence, and create a space internally for manifestation – 'Go within to go without.' Then, when the intentions have been set and the space created, we need to take action.

Linked to this is the ability to surrender to the flow and abundance of the universe. Releasing control is important, as this allows for opportunities and inspiration that we may not have foreseen.

## Perpetual transmutation of energy

This law describes how evolution is constantly happening. Everything is evolving. Our own cells regenerate completely every seven years, while every aspect of creation goes through a perpetual process of change. On an energetic level, things are being transmuted all the time, and some of it we don't even see.

This law can help us understand the mind, body and spirit connection better. Every action is preceded by a thought, and every thought has the power to create an action. If our physical health isn't up to par, our mental, emotional and spiritual health will suffer too. If we have issues with the way we think, feel and attempt to connect to a spiritual reality, our physical bodies will struggle to cope, which will result in ill-health. Everything is interconnected, and energy healers and practitioners recognize this, which is why we attempt to heal on the subtle and energetic planes of being as well as the physical.

Everything is in motion too, transmuting and changing all the time, which, in terms of being a psychic, is why it's important to keep your intuition intact. Intuition is like a muscle – it needs to be strengthened through use and given TLC for good health. Weak intuition prevents you from serving from the highest source and light. To sense the energetic blocks or wisdom and insight needing to come through and be known, you must be open to the concept of everything being in motion all the time, according to the Law of Perpetual Transmutation of Energy.

## Cause and effect

Quite simply, every action has consequences. That's the Law of Cause and Effect. Karma is linked to this universal law. Every action has a ripple effect – interconnectedness once more. What goes around comes around...

But so often we aren't conscious of how our past actions and beliefs are affecting us on an energetic level. Perhaps you were once in a position of power and misused that power, then at a later stage in life, someone has treated you in a less than favourable way and you feel disempowered.

The event causes you stress and anxiety, mild depression and potentially even health issues like insomnia or weight fluctuations, and you can't put your finger on why it happened. Sound familiar?

Consequences may present themselves months or years down the line. Time doesn't matter to karmic laws and the Law of Cause and Effect.

The key is that intention must accompany action, otherwise we would all be doomed from birth. Babies and children, for example, do things unconsciously, so it wouldn't be right to bind them to negative karma. Minor wrongdoings without conscious intention generally don't accumulate negative karma. But repetitive thoughts and actions with malicious intent, minor or major, do.

Also, on an internal level this law relates to the feelings and emotions we experience, such as the vibration and frequency of anger or resentment. Feeling jealous or resentful of someone's success, someone who hasn't caused us any harm, ultimately results in attracting that harm. This can further close us off from the level of fame, prestige, abundance, accomplishment or whatever else we are jealous of.

Treat others how you wish to be treated, in short. What you put or project out may not come back to you instantly, but it will come back eventually.

As a psychic and medium, it's especially important to work on your karma, so you don't keep attracting the same negative cycles or block your path to deeper connection and greater abundance.

## Compensation

It's important to know that all the universal laws are tied in closely to one another. We can see similarities and links or bridges between many of them. This one corresponds with the Law of Attraction and Law of Correspondence. It is a natural energy exchange similar to karmic law. You reap what you sow. What happens around you is a direct reflection of what happens within you. Positively, when you've reaped good karma, you are compensated by the universe. This is something to reflect on.

## Relativity

Did you know that comparison is actually a man-made concept? The true reality of divine oneness is that everything is neutral. We are in a world of duality – yin and yang, light and dark, masculine and feminine, good and bad, light and shadow, win and lose – yet the ultimate goal is always unity and harmony. There's a lesson in everything, and there's also a chance for unity.

Relativity comes down to how we choose to perceive things and interact with our physical world. When we compare without specific intentions, such as to evolve or

YOU MUST BE PSYCHIC

provide a framework for learning and transformation, self-improvement, etc., we create a polarity and division within ourselves. Furthermore, we create the reality of lack, loss or disappointment, feeling as if we never have enough, or we can't be content, or see the lesson and blessing in our situation. This disempowers us, so we can't take control of our own lives, leading to further disconnection from ourselves.

The Law of Relativity teaches us not to compare ourselves to others. The ego can divine, separate and distort, but the Higher Self unifies; this is where we celebrate our differences, finding strength and wisdom in others' talents and experiences. Comparison is unhealthy and self-destructive in the long run.

## Polarity

According to the Law of Polarity, everything has a light and a darkness to it, a positive and a negative, a masculine and a feminine, a yin and a yang. Polar opposites attract and repel, but eventually come together in unison. This is the main goal of the universe. It's also the main aim of our own bodies: to achieve equilibrium and internal harmony. All things wish to find unity, i.e. a unification and harmonization of polar opposites.

To be a psychic, medium or any other practitioner working with universal and spiritual energies, you must make peace with your divine feminine and divine masculine. This goes above and beyond human judgements; the divine feminine and divine masculine are innate energies based on the Law of Polarity. All men have an inner feminine; all women an inner masculine. Yin energy is feminine and magnetic, receptive and passive, while yang energy is masculine and electric, active and dominant. They 'flow' into each other in a rhythmic or cyclic motion.

## Rhythm

Cycles and natural patterns, natural rhythms, are found within our bodies, within the planet and within the universe. Seasons are an example of this, and women have periods or moon cycles. The Earth has cycles, too, and everything that occurs in the microcosm can be reflected in the macrocosm, and vice versa.

Emotions and inner energetic currents also follow the Law of Rhythm. Music and sound are linked to it too, so they are things you can work with in harmony with your intuitive and psychic gifts. Music and sound healing or therapy are great additions to your own well-being journey, as well as to your psychic services! Some of the best practitioners are those who have combined ancient sound healing techniques with the services they offer, such as having Tibetan singing bowls and chimes or a tribal drumming track as a background beat to their trance work.

YOU MUST BE PSYCHIC

The Law of Rhythm asks you to be honest with the natural rhythms that show up in your life, like your work, rest and play. Being a psychic takes incredible energy, as we explored in depth in the first chapter. Regardless of whether you're an empath or not, your innate rhythms and needs should be honoured, so you can be as good as you can be for yourself and others.

# Gender

Finally, the Law of Gender refers to the masculine and feminine energy within everything. Being a man or woman has nothing to do with masculine and feminine energy, although it is true that men are primarily masculine in nature and women are more feminine. In the 21st century, we've seen a rise in people identifying as non-binary or transgender. Some people say it's due to all the confusion and mixed messages coming from a consumerist global society. Others suggest it's a more natural and evolution-compatible process. In fact, both are true, or at least have the potential to be true, and this is a paradox in itself.

Duality and polarity run through all of life; thus, take what you need from this universal law. You might want to explore your feminine side if you're quite masculine (regardless of your gender) and you might wish to explore your masculine side if you're more feminine (regardless of your gender).

# The Higher Self: A direct link to psychic powers

If you wish to become a psychic, medium or spiritual healer of any kind, you must first develop a strong relationship with your Higher Self. Our Higher Self is the divine spark within us. It is connected with the universe, God, Divine Spirit or Source, or whatever you wish to name the higher power. It is self-aware and free from ego. Intuitive and psychic powers flow from the higher mind, thus it is essential to work with this aspect of ourselves.

Through our spiritual and psychic development, we can raise our vibration to access a higher state of consciousness, which brings us closer to Source. This simultaneously dissolves resistance to the flow of the universal laws, the awakening of dormant gifts and the development of transcendental awareness – the state of mind necessary for all sorts of empathic, super-sensitive and clairvoyant abilities to flow.

## The Higher Self and the soul

When this vast planetary exploration began, souls coming to Earth knew they were connected to Source. However, lifetime after lifetime, this innate wisdom diminished. We started to forget about our natural spiritual powers and became disconnected from our souls. Our vibrations became lower. Our spiritual frequencies became polluted. The ego took over, essentially, and intuitive, psychic and extra-sensory gifts and abilities were forgotten. Technology replaced them. Our connection to Source became weaker...

Thanks to this process, a reincarnated soul can become completely lost in the 3D matrix false reality timeline illusion, plagued by the negative karma from past lifetimes, and it seems to be trickier and trickier to evolve and transcend. Letting go of the shadow self and the wounds and traumas that accompany it can seem impossible. We also start to forget past lifetimes and the lessons learned when we refuse to do the inner work, let go of shadow traits and work on personal and collective karma.

It's not your job to heal every soul you meet or every incarnated spirit here on Earth. But it is your duty to heal yourself. Connecting with your Higher Self is an essential part of this, for the Higher Self acts as a bridge and portal to advanced and ascended channels of consciousness.

As we forgot our connection to Source, we felt isolated and became fearful. Honing and developing your psychic gifts can overcome this and restore that connection, so that you can feel supported and secure in the knowledge that you are not alone. Connecting with your Higher Self is one step towards wholeness and spiritual enlightenment. (*Remember there is an exercise for tuning into your Higher Self on page 44.*)

# Understanding your Etheric and Astral Bodies

As you have no doubt become aware, the path to becoming a real-life psychic or medium involves a certain level of self-knowledge. As well as connecting with your Higher Self, you should also be aware of your etheric and astral bodies. These are the 'extensions' of your soul print, or your soul's energetic blueprint. Let's look at all the bodies now.

## The physical body

This is the very physical and tangible body you reside in. It is responsible for holding sensory data and information and interacting with your emotional and mental bodies. During meditation, the universal life-force energy of *chi* stimulates this process, as does psychic energy. Your physical body is essentially a transmitter and receiver of all the information coming in from the mental, emotional, astral and spiritual planes.

## The etheric body

Your etheric body is located just above and beyond your physical body and creates a channel between the physical and the astral. This body can be seen as an energetic blueprint for the physical body, as it is a subtle replica of it. It transmits data and sensory information, including information about your physical health and the vibratory state of health of each of your subtle bodies. If you are suffering with physical ailments, a lot of psychic impressions will be coming through the etheric body. Healing can be given to that body and the effects will ripple downwards into the physical too.

## The astral body

This body is the link to the subconscious and spiritual aspects and dimensions of being. It picks up on and stores all the sensations, memories, stories, experiences, emotions, interactions and observations of your lifetime. Ill-health, distortions and imbalances are included here.

Key insights into your beliefs, feelings, emotions, thoughts and deepest desires are transmitted through your astral body. It is also the body used for astral projection and travel and for receiving ancient wisdom and inspiration in dreams. Your astral body is a gateway to your spiritual body.

## The spiritual body

Your spiritual body is a direct link to the divine, higher or cosmic consciousness and the angelic and light realms. Everything 'above and beyond' our three-dimensional human reality can be experienced and accessed through this body. It is a bridge between the human and the divine, and it's essential for accessing psychic and mediumistic abilities.

As the mind, body, emotions and spirit are all intrinsically connected, cleansing and purifying your physical body also cleanses and purifies your other bodies. So, I would advise doing a fast or detox from time to time. Fasts and detoxes can lighten you and connect you to more subtle expressions of being. It may be a very simple analogy, but picture a feather next to a stone. Of course, the feather will be lifted more easily by a gust of wind. Nature's breeze will allow it to float and even move around, while the stone will remain still and stuck. Psychic energy can be seen as nature's breeze.

# 9

# THE SHADOW SELF, WOUNDS AND TRAUMA

Unlike the Higher Self, which connects us to the divine and is a holy source of inspiration and personal power, the shadow self is the part of human nature often considered impure, dark and undesirable. It is the repressed part, made up of everything we reject or seek to deny. It can be formed of completely unconscious behaviours and patterns. Sexuality can be part of it, but it can also include things like not wanting to make money from our gifts or staying stuck in 'poverty consciousness' – a state of lack, feeling that we have to suffer.

There is also a collective shadow which may affect us in certain ways; essentially, we take on part of it, along with the responsibility of transcending it.

If we look at astrology, we can see that:

- Aries needs to transcend ego, narcissism and bullying tendencies to move towards their light self of confidence, leadership and courage.
- Taurus needs to transcend lethargy, stubbornness and excessive materialism to move towards their light self of benevolence, compassion, trustworthiness and dependability.
- Gemini needs to transcend gossip, manipulation and superficiality to move towards their light self of intellectualism, quick wit, excellent communication and potent imagination.
- Cancer needs to transcend moodiness, pessimism and manipulative tendencies to move towards their light self of imaginative and spiritual powers, potent instincts and amazing intuition.
- Leo needs to transcend false pride, self-centredness and narcissism to move towards their light self of extraordinary charm, creative inspiration and leadership.
- Virgo needs to transcend self-criticism, perfectionism and intellectual superiority to move towards their light self of potent responsibility, emotional intelligence and compassion for themselves and others.
- Libra needs to transcend superficiality, indecision and people-pleasing to move towards their light

self of creating harmony and peace and being a diplomat and a beautifully balanced being.

- Scorpio needs to transcend vindictiveness, possessiveness and manipulation to move towards their light self of spiritual power and intuition, empathy and potent imaginative and artistic gifts.
- Sagittarius needs to transcend self-righteousness, arrogance and aggression to move towards their light self of honesty, commitment to higher truth and idealistic vision.
- Capricorn needs to transcend emotional suppression, being a control freak and being over-concerned with status, money and image to move towards their light self of discipline, self-control and spiritual and material synergy.
- Aquarius needs to transcend rebellion, emotional aloofness and a lack of empathy and kindness to move towards their light self of being an altruistic humanitarian with a powerful intellect and intuition and friendliness.
- Pisces needs to transcend weak boundaries, pessimism and over-giving and trusting tendencies to move towards their light self of an unconditionally loving, kind and selfless creative genius and spiritual master.

So, the collective shadow is actually a route to higher consciousness, as well as self-knowledge, if we choose to see it that way. We are multi-dimensional and holistic beings, who must work through our wounds and shadows to find the light. For now, please be aware of how denial or repression of both your personal and the collective shadow can lead to more of what you don't want. Imagine trying to push two of the same polarities of a magnet together; they just keep repelling each other. Well, the more you try to deny or reject core parts of yourself, the more you embody or become them. To transcend them instead, remember this mantra: 'In and out, up and through.'

It is good to remember that some aspects of ourselves that we may wish to deny are inescapable. We all have basic needs, in addition to survival instincts, primal desires and a human body. We all have an ego and a psyche. But this doesn't mean that we should remain in self-denial or a state of illusion. If we look at it from a different perspective, accepting and embracing our shadow can lead to more of what we do want, that is, our light or positive attributes.

If we take the collective shadow wound of sexuality, for example, something we all have a tricky time with at some point in our lives, navigating our way through strong emotions, vulnerabilities, desires and needs for intimacy and romance, we can see that denying these wants and needs puts us in a state of suffering. Over time, self-esteem diminishes, family and friendship relationships can break down, and chaos is caused on multiple levels, in many life areas. This is a simple example, but a real one.

To take an individual shadow example, a Pisces Sun sign person denying that they have weak boundaries and are over-giving and over-trusting may lead to lots of problems, including but not limited to falling into loneliness, isolation and apathy.

In this respect, accepting and integrating elements of our shadow self can lead to the things we may originally think can only be attained by suppressing the shadow and focusing solely on the light. We are governed by both light and darkness, day and night, sunshine and moonlight, and positive and negative forces. Something may be seen as dark due to its feminine or yin-like nature, but it doesn't mean it can't be turned into something light.

The same is true for the ego; the ego can be a direct path to higher self-awareness and amazing psychic gifts. It's only when we get stuck or lost in it that it becomes bad. The ego is actually essential and we wouldn't get anything done without it driving our everyday human existence. It just needs to be balanced, which means there needs to be a harmonization and unification of our shadow and light qualities.

As a healer or psychic, it's your job to be honest about yourself and accountable for your actions. That way you can integrate your shadow and embody more light. Then you can become a powerful change-maker and guide for others.

# Rising Above the Shadow

We have the power within us to transcend the limitations of our shadow. So, no matter how hard life gets or how many challenges there are, please don't ever let the world turn you cold. Take this advice. Don't be steered off your path by the injustices, coldness or harshness of the world. You will undoubtedly meet some cold and narcissistic characters, as we discussed earlier (*see page 24*), and people can certainly break our heart, diminish our confidence and destroy our self-esteem, momentarily. But people can also lift us up, inspire us and gently nudge us along our path to becoming the beautiful healer or teacher we are meant to be.

Multiple choices define our fates, therefore it's your job and duty to stay strong and heal your personal shadow. Your wounds don't define you, they are just there to shape and redirect you. You have free will, yet you also have a destiny... If it's your destiny as an incarnated being here on this marvellous planetary Earth timeline to be a healer or psychic, then you will be. You just need to remember the power of making conscious choices in each moment.

We'll always have a shadow, both personal and collective. We'll always have an ego with its needs and desires of body and mind. However, fortunately there are many beings of the light who will show up on our path to inspire and help us. Our Higher Self is always available. Finally, when a soul chooses a body, it makes a conscious choice to experience life on Earth with specific parents, family and other members of a soul group, from strangers to lovers and animals to friends. An individual soul agrees to experience certain life events in order to learn and develop spiritually, thus becoming closer to God/Spirit/Source. But this can only occur when we are in tune with our Higher Self and spirit body, so remember this if you ever find yourself falling into denial or delusion. Spoken with love.

# 10

# ARCHANGELS, SPIRIT ANIMALS AND YOUR PERSONAL TEAM

Each of us has a team of spirit helpers. This can include angels, spirit guides, spirit animals and loved ones. We don't necessarily have to have known them in our physical life. I believe these helpers are assigned to us before we are born.

I also believe in angels and that each of us can invoke their assistance.

## Archangels

In traditional Christianity, archangels are among those who carry out the most important tasks of God. Many religions, cultures and individuals have reported appearances of angelic figures. These have come through visions, dreams, meditation, near-death experiences or moments of realization of our divine and interconnected nature.

Archangels show themselves to people who genuinely need help. They exist on multiple planes of existence and are close to Source energy because they have transcended the egotistical games and follies of the lower human mind. They are beings who have ascended to the higher heights; they have fully balanced, integrated and embodied the qualities of universal compassion, unconditional love, tolerance, patience, empathy, benevolence, supreme kindness and generosity, and non-judgement. The seven archangels that I would like to present to you here are: Raphael, Michael, Gabriel, Uriel, Jophiel, Zadkiel and Haniel.

## Archangel Raphael

Archangel Raphael is charged with overseeing the healing of all the people on Earth. He is connected to a feminine energy that brings love, compassion and radiant light to those he heals. Actually known as 'He who heals', he is full of grace, tolerance, patience, empathy and wisdom. He himself has experienced the trials and tribulations of the human path, so he understands the struggles, challenges and difficult decisions we face. He has also been on a deep and authentic journey to transcend, heal and move past the 'lower vibrations' that come with life on Earth. Earth is a game, to some degree. There are many levels, which all humans can reach, and as Raphael has reached them, he is one of the best way-showers for us.

Light and dark are forces that all the angels have mastered, but Raphael takes this to a new mode of excellency. He is a light-bringer of the highest order, so is the perfect archangel to call on if you need healing. Through elevated compassion, tolerance and understanding, he creates internal shifts in those he touches, smoothing out emotional, physical, psychological and spiritual blocks and imbalances. He shines a healing light on our fears, insecurities, doubts, worries and blocks, bringing love, happiness, good health, longevity and abundance. He is a divine channel and guiding light for many, and you can ask for his assistance at any time to overcome pain.

Raphael is also known as the angel of healers! He works specifically with healers, therapists, nurses, physicians, counsellors, practitioners of herbal medicine and spiritual healers. He is a voice for all those who heal others. If you fall into this category, Raphael will give you the boost you need to carry out your tasks and offer your services at a higher level. He has been described as 'the medicine god' and 'healing energy of the divine', and is usually shown as carrying a staff with a caduceus on it. This is the ancient symbol of the medical arts. Sometimes he is depicted as having a travelling pilgrim next to him with a staff in one hand and bowl of healing ointment or balm in the other, signifying his secondary role: he heals and protects travellers...

In full, Raphael's role includes:

- Providing healing and comfort to those who are sick, mentally, physically, emotionally or spiritually.
- Giving guidance and support to all doctors, healers, nurses, apothecaries and health institutions.
- Healing those who are plagued by dark forces, 'demons', destructive energy and negative thoughts, leading to depression or a number of health issues.
- Providing healing and protection to travellers. If you're a regular traveller, a digital nomad or are planning on taking a trip, perhaps overseas, Raphael can help you travel safely. He ensures journeys go smoothly without hiccups or failures. His healing light helps us all to avoid failures, setbacks and accidents linked to movement.
- Raphael also assists us in releasing trapped energy, blocked emotions and trauma and wounds that we are unconsciously holding on to. His Emerald Green Ray can help us further.

## Archangel Raphael's Emerald Green Ray

This increases life-force energy, physical vitality and longevity. It is linked to the heart chakra. As the embodiment of healing, universal love and compassion, Raphael activates this chakra, awakening our innate gifts and qualities and unblocking our beautiful energetic flow. He aligns us with the benevolent powers of the spiritual universe, putting us on a brighter and better path, and connecting us to our own sense of vision, so higher power flows to us in abundance.

He may oversee all beings on Earth, but we can create a personal connection to him through intention, purity and communication. (We'll look at communicating with the archangels later in this chapter.)

You may notice that Raphael is referred to as 'he'. Generally speaking, people have interpreted angels' and archangels' gender in a variety of ways. I would personally suggest it doesn't matter. On the subtle, spiritual and higher planes, all is love and oneness. Unity consciousness prevails and purity replaces gender relevance.

## Archangel Michael

Archangel Michael, also known as Saint Michael, is a spiritual warrior of truth and justice. He is one of the best-known archangels, because he is very powerful and protects a lot of people. He is a champion of the underdog, fighting demons and striving for righteousness in the battle of good vs evil. Whether you take biblical translations literally or metaphorically, Michael fights for justice and truth in a way that makes him an angel of the highest order. Traditionally depicted wearing armour and holding a sword, a banner or scales, he is seen as the chief of the angels, a commanding presence who deserves respect. He conquers demons and is believed to have battled Satan himself.

Michael embodies a potent spiritual energy and is the guardian of all who need protection and guidance, so you can call on him for help with anything from the most mundane to the most serious of issues. He will appear to you when you have lost faith, hope or inspiration. He reminds you of the power of good, purity, righteousness, grace and unwavering determination – determination to rise from the depths of evil into the light.

His sword often appears to those on a spiritual path or to anyone who has activated their third eye chakra, engages in frequent meditation and keeps the faith. This sword is a timeless symbol of conquering darkness, evil and injustice, even down to the petty nuisances and disagreements that are the result of someone's ignorance or extreme stubbornness. Of course, when we have suffered a major injustice relating to money, security, love, home or family life, career or our right to good health and prosperity or protection, Archangel Michael will also step in.

As a saint, he has worked through his own imbalances and toxicity and reached an elevated status. He is fully aware of the light and dark parts of humankind, as well as the evil that can be committed by an out-of-control ego. He shines light on chaos and destruction, whether individual or global, as he has been charged with the task of restoring order and divine justice to the earthly realm. To do this, he works in many dimensions and on many timelines too – his love really is infinite!

He observes human antics and hears people's calls for help, and is happy to assist, as long as the prayer or cry for help is sincere. In other words, it needs to be rooted in genuine distress, such as being heartbroken or conned, or suffering family, pet or soulmate loss, rather than just being a bid for attention. Archangel Michael is actually here to help us uncover BS and deception and heal from loss and pain. He oversees all life on Earth without judgement and with total compassion and empathy, and restores faith, hope, divine law and order, love, harmony, peace and serenity.

In fact, Michael's duties are vast, so much so that I have personally formed an intimate connection with him to learn more. He has helped me be more empathic when I've lost vision, and in the brief moments when I've let myself be overcome by judgement (the ego).

I've found that Archangel Michael provides a vision of his sword to let us know that it's OK to cut through the BS and illusions. We aren't meant to live in ignorance or fear – this is something I have also learned on my journey. Michael can protect us while bringing a higher truth.

With his help, we can see more clearly and uncover the mysteries of our own beliefs and behaviours as well as the beliefs and behaviours of others. He shows up (or can be called on) when we find out that people have been lying to us or have wronged us. It's not right to be treated like dirt, or as an emotional dumping ground. Michael stands for fairness and justice on every level, even if it ruffles some feathers. He is a cosmic pot-stirrer, but a righteous one with a high sense of integrity.

Overall, Michael is a spiritual warrior who will bring out our own inner spiritual warrior. We can work with him through prayer and meditation to increase our own capacity to help others. Becoming more intuitive, alert for hidden manipulations and false motives, spiritually aware, faithful and self-assured is part of this, as is trusting in a higher power.

Michael also brings comfort and assurance in a way that lets us know, without a shadow of a doubt, that it's OK to stand up to violence. Abuse, slander, treachery, immoral behaviour and preying on people's kindness are included in this. If you've ever been conned, abused or taken advantage of in a major way, Michael's love and light will guide you back to your legacy. He sparks your soul mission.

Other key strengths given and received include protection, courage, self-esteem, guidance, emotional balance, good health, enlightenment, healing abilities, serenity, purification and divine inspiration. Call on Archangel Michael the holy protector and he will help you move from depression and despair to self-worth, confidence and clarity – with your spiritual vision intact! He's a powerful ally to have.

## Archangel Gabriel

Archangel Gabriel, whose name means 'God is my Strength', is the angel of communication, creativity and inspiration. Known as 'the divine messenger', she represents heavenly protection, peace, harmony and self-empowerment. She is a beautifully serene and protective angel with a heart of gold.

Gabriel is a spiritual leader known to help with communication, clarity and authenticity, so you can call on her if you're a writer, author, speaker, publisher, poet, singer, coach, counsellor, manager, entertainer, leader or guide (of any kind), or work in any field which requires excellent communication. If you're working towards becoming a professional psychic, medium or spiritual healer, Gabriel is the perfect archangel for you, as she can assist with empathy, mindfulness and imagination, as well as logic, higher reasoning and cerebral analysis. With her help, your communication skills can skyrocket, which will help with manifesting abundance, peace and beauty.

Archangel Gabriel is also the angel to call on for inspiration for artistic, musical and other creative endeavours and projects. Secondly, she can be called on for healing, counselling and therapeutic pursuits, as long as your voice is involved.

If you have enthusiasm, passion and zest for a project, vocation, profession or service, Gabriel will amplify these positive feelings. She brings nurturing and supportive energy and strength, assertion and confidence in equal measure. Being a female archangel with immense strength and clarity, she herself has balanced energy.

So, creative vision, infinite possibility and potential, and a connection to subconscious wisdom, messages and inspiration are all available with Gabriel. Her healing light is pure, sensual and majestic. She is here to align us with self-mastery, the mastery of our gifts and the realization of our potential and ability to create, manifest and evolve.

Gabriel is usually seen with a trumpet, and often in a setting with other musical instruments or ensembles. The trumpet is a symbol of being welcomed into the heavenly gates. Metaphorically, it signifies harnessing our gifts and qualities to receive the protection and abundance we need. In general, the more we connect with archangels, the more we can live our best life.

White feathers are also symbolic of Gabriel's presence. If she shows herself to us repeatedly through sacred symbols like these, we might be destined to create a masterpiece! If we need help with art, music, inspiration, creative projects or speaking of any kind, of course we can actively ask for her assistance. All she asks of us is that we are honest about our soul's talents and how we can present them to the world.

It's all about self-expression, the blissful flow of fresh perspectives and new insights leading to magic and creations that serve the soul... Gabriel is an archangel who is very supportive of unique and out-the-box ideas, as long as they're rooted in a genuine desire to serve humanity in some way. She inspires and encourages us to unleash our creativity on the world with sensitivity and confidence. Her message: 'Stay strong, speak your truth and use your voice with sensitivity and confidence.'

In essence, Gabriel is a champion of empathic, mindful and authentic communication. She guides us to put care and thought into the words we use and how we deliver them. Language, speech and music are important! They can be used to destroy or create, cause chaos or heal, and spark distortion and disconnection or unite people in loving harmony. Positive, loving and kind self-talk is also linked to Gabriel.

Gabriel has a healing energy and presence that grants permission to shy or reserved folk to live up to their full potential. This is excellent news for empaths. Gabriel can help motivate you into greatness in your personal, profes-sional and community life; she dispels any fear of shining or speaking and brings the motivation to succeed.

Ultimately, Gabriel is the best archangel to call on for all matters of communication, public speaking and self-expression, including professional projects that require a beautiful or eloquent voice. She is linked to the white and golden light of the crown chakra and these are the colour frequencies you can visualize, work with and meditate on for connection and contact with her.

# Archangel Uriel

Archangel Uriel is the angel of wisdom who is also known as 'the light of God', 'God's truth', 'fire of God' and 'angel of presence'. He offers wisdom, information and solutions to challenges in the most divine of ways. He is the archangel to work with when you want to deepen your studies, expand your horizons and become an expert in your chosen field. He is seen as carrying a book or scroll, which symbolizes wisdom.

Uriel is known as the angel who protected the Tree of Life with his flaming sword. Alongside Raphael, Michael and Gabriel, he is one of the angels protecting the four corners of the globe – Raphael the west, Michael the east, Gabriel the north, and Uriel the south. This makes him very important in our healing endeavours.

Uriel shines a light on God's truth, bringing to awareness the importance of resolving conflicts and tensions built on drama or disagreements. He is here to bring deeper awareness, self-knowledge and understanding to the earthly realm. He wants people to live in peace, coupled with higher truth and wisdom.

To achieve this, we have to be open to healing, higher wisdom and conflict resolution. This means losing the stubbornness that many of us often hold on to and being much more adaptable, flexible and open-minded. Holding on to grudges, seeking revenge or being possessive and fixated on ideas, people and outgrown stories isn't good for us.

Through the wisdom he offers, Uriel steers us into releasing toxic or self-limiting stories and embracing our Higher Self and our soul mission.

As well as his book or scroll, Uriel has the secondary symbol of an open hand holding a flame or the sun, which is said to represent God's truth.

In recognizing our capacity for ancient wisdom, Higher Self-awareness and intuition, Uriel helps us to feel more empowered. He brings inspiration, self-respect, self-assurance and the advancement of psychic gifts. Oh yes, psychic gifts are connected to Archangel Uriel. He can help us with unravelling ancient mysteries and accessing forbidden knowledge and memories from past lives.

Uriel's primary colour is red, the colour of passion, self-preservation and grounding. His secondary colour is yellow, the colour of wisdom, self-empowerment, self-esteem, ambition and personal authority. Red links to the root chakra and yellow to the solar plexus – something to keep in mind! Through embracing the ultimate truths that Uriel illuminates, you can become more accomplished and assured, as well as transparent in your dealings. This is how your professional, personal and social life soar...

## Archangel Jophiel

Jophiel is a female archangel symbolizing the beauty of the soul, and her name means 'Beauty of God'. She asks us to let go of shallowness and superficiality and focus on inner beauty and sensuality. She will protect and guide you if you're a sensitive soul dealing with narcissistic characters! She will shine a light on the unkindness and selfishness of those around you, so you can refine your strength, and will enhance the warmth and sensitivity in your heart, without allowing you to fall into self-sacrifice. Think back to the first chapter, where I went through the qualities of an empath; boundaries are important. Actually they're essential. Jophiel will help you to maintain them and transcend sacrifice. That *isn't* essential.

Jophiel also encourages depth and intimacy on a soul level. So, looking in the mirror every day with a smug look, saying, 'Who's the fairest of them all?' is not advised. Don't get me wrong – there's nothing wrong with healthy self-worth, or valuing physical beauty. But inner beauty should always come first. Jophiel can give our auric field a boost that will encourage deeper intimacy in both romantic and Platonic relationships.

Gratitude, appreciation and grace are further gifts that Jophiel can give. She will help us to see the beauty in others, in our own soul and in our surroundings. Warm, sensual and elegant herself, she inspires these qualities in others, as well as optimism and positivity.

Emotional intelligence, depth, sensitivity, vulnerability and wisdom are also part of Jophiel's healing light. Breakthroughs, including seeing through the veil of illusion, self-discovery, sharing wisdom acquired through life experience and hardships and transforming negative and pessimistic belief systems into inspiration and motivation are part of Jophiel's domain. She heals negative emotions, chaotic situations and relationships or encounters that have brought nothing but disparity and confusion, and she instils peace, serenity and contentment into our minds and hearts.

Jophiel's Yellow Ray of light will purify any chaos in our lives. It can help us eliminate distractions and rise up into a more illuminated and self-aware space.

Moreover, the high-vibrational energy that Jophiel brings helps us achieve creative and spiritual greatness. Divine inspiration, linked to unique art, music and clarity of mind and perception, becomes available to us.

In addition to actively calling on Jophiel through evoking her Yellow Ray, you will sense her presence through seeing yellow or golden-yellow orbs or rays of light. These can appear in waking life or in dreams.

## Archangel Zadkiel

Archangel Zadkiel is the angel of benevolence, freedom and mercy. He teaches how to forgive, have mercy and practise benevolence on a deep level. He comes into our lives to create shifts when people have wronged us or we need freedom from unhealthily binding stories and are holding on to the grief, pain and trauma of heartbreak or betrayal.

When we can't forgive, we only create pain and struggle for ourselves and those around us. Lack of forgiveness is the precursor to lasting resentments, health issues, money blocks and an inability to let love or friendship flow.

Every conflict has more than one party involved, otherwise it wouldn't be a conflict! As the angel of mercy, Zadkiel shows the way to the highest expressions of human forgiveness and self-accountability. Call on him if you wish to cleanse emotional toxins from your sacral and heart chakras, build healthier relationships and connect to Source energy.

Zadkiel is usually depicted holding a blade or dagger and fighting the forces of evil. Known as 'the righteousness of God' or 'the grace of God', he is connected to the Violet Flame, which is linked to the divine alchemical powers of transformation and is a part of a unique initiation often presented in the Reiki healing system. In terms of light healing rays, his colour is violet.

We can call on Zadkiel or connect with him in prayer or meditation to transmute darkness, transform challenging areas of our lives and find freedom.

He helps us to find our inner flame and activates our third eye chakra, which is the seat of vision, intuition and extra-sensory gifts. Violet is the colour of the third eye.

If there's something preventing us from enjoying freedom, like fears or insecurities, Zadkiel will cut through them like a blade through a piece of paper. He aids in overcoming obstacles, seeing through self-created fears or illusions and achieving magical transformations.

Self-fulfilling prophecies can be overcome with Zadkiel's divine assistance. These are essentially repeating a negative story or belief to the point of it coming true. Archangel Zadkiel encourages forgiving both ourselves and others, and releasing judgements that foster hatred or negativity. To encourage us, he sparks memories of our divine nature, as well as of the good in others.

Getting to the root of our spiritual origins through exploring our past is part of his domain too. He enables deep self-discovery, coupled with soul-searching and unearthing memories long forgotten, including of psychic gifts we may once have been shielded from, perhaps because we weren't ready or would have reacted from ego or greed, or fallen into despair and depression. Through self-healing and psychic development, with Zadkiel's help, we become more conscious of such memories, recalling them in meditation or dreams. This can lead to clearing internal blockages on multiple planes and fields and remembering our soul purpose or life's mission.

Compassion, forgiveness, emotional harmony, relationship synergy, positive mirroring or self-reflection, and letting go of deep trauma and emotional pain are all part of the assistance Zadkiel can provide. He also helps to clear old karmic debts and remove negative energy from our aura, releasing anger and the feelings of victimhood, so we don't repeat negative karmic cycles that circulate hate, jealousy, ignorance, fear and a lack of sensitivity, depth and soul. Karmic release on a soul level is part of his duties, hence the dagger or blade; he cuts through karmic contracts in the most magnificent of ways.

Moreover, he inspires respect for our brothers and sisters, brings the realization that we are one interconnected global family, and promotes tolerance and diplomacy at saint-like levels. Personally, he encourages us to take steps towards recovery, healing and enlightenment, as well as adopting self-care routines that bring us peace and serenity.

## Archangel Haniel

Another archangel to work with for peace and serenity is Haniel. She is one of the female angels representing intuition, joy, pleasure, sensuality and the feminine qualities of the moon and Venus. She is known as 'the angel of joy' and 'the angel of pleasure'. She can be called on and connected to for help with developing our instincts, intuition and divine feminine wisdom.

While Raphael symbolizes the divine masculine light and wisdom, Haniel symbolizes the female energy of God's grace. Her name itself translates as 'Joy of God', therefore she can help with all aspects of depression, lethargy, loneliness, isolation and being stuck in a rut. She is here to help us be joyful and connect to the simple pleasures of life. Her message is one of happiness, laughter and positivity – and remaining optimistic even through the hard times.

All the beautiful qualities of Venus and the moon come through Haniel. Venus symbolizes female sexuality, pleasure, romance, beauty and sensuality. The moon represents instincts, magnetism, receptivity, passivity, nurturing, gentleness, compassion, emotions, sacred knowledge, ancient wisdom and spiritual powers.

So, Haniel shows us how to be more sensitive, empathic and self-aware, as well as how to connect to the spiritual and raw emotional power of the universe. Inner currents and sensations that lead to divine inspiration and enhanced self-knowledge are energized by her presence. We can become more conscious of the invisible energy that connects everything and everyone.

Haniel has a gentle yet firm touch. She reminds us to be loving, but have healthy boundaries, so we don't fall into servitude or self-sacrifice. For those who may naturally have a feminine disposition, and perhaps be overly submissive and yielding, she is the angel to call on for additional strength. People-pleasing, appeasing and sacrificial tendencies can be transcended!

Simultaneously, Haniel sparks divine femininity in those who need to embody greater sensitivity and gentleness, also the ability to go with the flow, think imaginatively and see things from a spiritual perspective.

Simply put, her message is to follow your highest joy. Embrace your passions, your need for sensual self-expression and the inner intuitive and emotional forces that guide you to love, friendship and intimacy. Dance, music and sound, combined with imaginative pathways to happiness, are key to Haniel's teaching.

Ultimately, Haniel represents unconditional love, sensitivity and divine feminine wisdom that can spark spiritual and sacred awareness. She helps us to balance yin and yang, feminine and masculine energies, so we can live our best life. If you struggle with aggression, competitiveness, a need to dominate others (at unhealthy levels) or excessive masculine energy, Haniel will assist you in restoring balance. She alleviates some of the unruly and destructive attributes of Mars, the planet of war, aggression, lust, dominance and vitality. Energy, passion and vitality are essential, but too much of them and Venus' beautiful qualities are squished!

Furthermore, Haniel helps with recovery from deep pain, trauma and heartache. Family or career loss, heartbreak, trauma and painful memories that refuse to budge can all be eased and soothed with her assistance. She teaches us that joy is our birthright and we don't need to hold on to fears, wounds, grief, shame, blame, resentment, hatred, denial or anger. These block lasting happiness, peace and even longevity. With Haniel's healing light, though, emotions that limit and hinder us can be harmonized, balanced and released with grace and integrity. Additionally, co-dependency, sexual and emotional blocks and wounds, and stagnation in our friendship, family, romantic, professional and social lives can be brought to her light for cleansing.

# Communication with the Archangels

Communication with the archangels can be achieved through aura strengthening and protecting and third eye activation. How does this work? Our aura transmits and receives signals and messages from the physical, emotional, mental, astral, spiritual and soul planes. Everything in this conscious universe is able to be transmitted and received, but it is essential to have an open third eye chakra for such phenomena to come through. The third eye is known as the seat of vision, intuition and the higher mind. Without an open and active third eye, we won't be able to perceive subtle energy, come to terms with new concepts or universal truths, or be open to such magical frequencies as messages from the archangels.

## Third eye activation

You can't expect to receive the infinite blessings and wisdom of the universe if you're closed off spiritually, and your third eye chakra is a bridge to such blessings. It's a channel connecting you to the quantum spiritual world.

To activate it, try the exercise below with any of these crystals: amethyst, angelite, azurite, celestite, clear quartz, lapis lazuli or sodalite. The key here is to combine visualization, inner knowing, intuition, trust and transcendental self-awareness with strong intentions.

- Begin by getting into your meditative space, taking deep breaths...
- Mentally construct a protective pyramid around you. The pyramid is symbolic of the three, the Holy Trinity. The pyramids of Giza were created based on ancient knowledge regarding sacred geometry, as were other temple pyramids around the world. Just as colours carry a unique frequency, so do shapes!
- Bring your chosen crystal up to your third eye, in the centre of your forehead.
- Lightly tap it against your forehead, visualizing healing energy sparking from it.
- Then gently rub it in a circular motion on your third eye.
- Connect to it and its healing properties on an energetic level. You can program and project intentions into it while rubbing it against your third eye. Essentially, you are activating your psychic centre through the connection with the crystal.

This exercise is simple yet highly effective. It strengthens your mental abilities and shields you from psychic attack.

It amplifies your aura and sparks soul remembrance – remembrance of your destiny and life purpose on a deep level. You can contemplate the mind, body and spirit connection, reflect on your past, and create powerful intentions for your future. It's an amazing way to connect with the loving intentions, compassion and healing of your spirit team too.

## Crystal water or elixirs

Another powerful way to raise your inner vibration, which simultaneously sparks your receptivity to the spirit world, is to make crystal water or elixirs. This is both fun and really empowering.

A small crystal which has been cleansed can purify water, clearing it of any ethereal pollution and psychic impurities that it has picked up. Detoxifying your system with crystal water can really relieve you of any psychic impurities too, while strengthening your auric field and helping you become more open to angelic assistance.

Crystal elixirs are an ancient therapy going back to Atlantean and ancient Egyptian times. Many cultures had temples made from crystals and rare gemstones, because they were aware of their healing properties and powers. Ayurvedic medicine, which originated in India, also uses crystals; gems are ground into a very fine powder and mixed with liquid, which the patient then takes at prescribed dosages. Boiling gemstones in spring water can also produce gem remedies; the gem is then removed and the water is diluted to make the remedy.

As you are aware by now, crystals embody unique vibrational frequencies that interact with our own electro-magnetic energy fields in profound ways. When we meditate or consciously connect to a crystal, its aura vibrates in synergy with ours, allowing its amazing healing qualities to positively affect us. The same is true for crystal water.

However, it is important to note that not all crystals can be used in this way. The best crystal to use is clear quartz, due to its link to all the chakras and subtle bodies and its amplifying and energizing effects. You can also use any crystal whose healing properties you require, but first make sure you check with a professional such as a crystal thera-pist or reputable online resource, as it is dangerous to consume certain crystals.

## Crystal water

- To begin, first cleanse your crystal (*see page 118*) and charge it (*page 121*) with your intentions and loving, healing thoughts.
- The crystal should be placed in the bottom of a non-metallic container and filled with spring, mineral, mountain, purified or reverse osmosis water. Ideally, not tap water unless you live in an amazing place!
- You should leave it there for twelve hours.

- If the container is glass, you can place it in natural
  sunlight for 12–24 hours, which gives it an extra boost.
  For feminine stones, you can leave the crystal-infused
  water in moonlight.

Crystal water needs to be drunk within one to three days if
kept outside a fridge or within a few weeks if in a fridge.

You can build up your auric defences by drinking a few
glassfuls of crystal water every day.

## The benefits of crystal water

Crystal water:
- Removes toxins and impurities from the bloodstream
- Neutralizes mental distortions and alleviates
  distorted and faulty beliefs and blockages
- Releases inner frequencies that have become
  muddied with toxic mindsets or behaviours
- Helps to protect you from negative energy,
  psychic attack and electromagnetic harm
- Strengthens the immune system to build up the
  body's defences against colds and flu
- Amplifies other essences and tonics such as flower
  essences, vitamins and herbal elixirs
- Provides energy, vitality and clear sight
- Sparks intuitive and psychic abilities

- Activates consciousness through its link to the subtle energy bodies
- Awakens dormant gifts, hidden memories and ancient wisdom linked to the multi-dimensional planes.

## Gem essences

Gem essences work like flower or herbal essences and elixirs, and can positively restructure your DNA and change your energetic blueprint, while having a cyclic and re-energizing effect. They're a daily dose of vibration-raising drops of consciousness. (*For the best gems to use, see the weekly plan on page 242.*)

To make a gem essence:

- Create gem water in the same way as crystal water, leaving your gemstone in the water for 12 hours. (Drinking gem water is an excellent way of becoming aware of the healing properties of different gems.)
- Then, mix the gem water with alcohol, preferably pure vodka. The combination should be 50:50.

Add 4–5 drops of gem essence to a glass of spring water or a chemical-free cold drink and sip at intervals throughout the day.

Your gem essence can be kept in tincture bottles for up to 6 months.

You can also dowse with a pendulum to find out:

1. Which essence(s) you require. Place your gem essence bottles in a group and ask whether there is a gem essence in the group that is needed. You may find you're guided to more than one essence.
2. How many doses you require. Ask how many days the essence should be taken for, using questions that allow for a 'yes' or 'no' answer, for instance, 'Should I take this essence once, twice, thrice, etc?'

When taking gem essences, the benefits can be reduced if you are consuming substances that alter the body's metabolism, like coffee, tea, alcohol or cigarettes or pharmaceutical drugs. If you are taking a homoeopathic remedy, do not take gem essences until the course of treatment is complete.

## Care to get creative?

If you like, you can create a gem essence for each day of the week. Each day corresponds to a planet, which has its own energetic symbolism and qualities. Here is a weekly plan of gem essences:

| | |
|---|---|
| **SUNDAY** | • Sunday is associated with the sun, including the qualities of dominance, will-power, self-esteem, ambition, creativity, vitality, prosperity, success, energy, positivity, renewal, strength and good luck.<br>• *Crystals for Sunday:* Amber, carnelian, citrine, clear quartz, green aventurine, peridot, red jasper, rose quartz, sapphire, sunstone, tiger's eye and topaz |
| **MONDAY** | • Monday is associated with moon, including the qualities of empathy, emotional intelligence, nurturing, caring, compassion, sensitivity, sacred knowledge, imagination, instincts, feelings and the subconscious mind.<br>• *Crystals for Monday:* Amethyst, aquamarine, carnelian, celestite, moonstone, pearl, selenite, smoky quartz, sugilite and tiger's eye |
| **TUESDAY** | • Tuesday is associated with Mars, including the qualities of passion, vitality, competition, action, a warrior mindset, masculine sexuality, will, ambition and enthusiasm.<br>• *Crystals for Tuesday:* Bloodstone, garnet, haematite, jet, moldavite, obsidian, ruby, sapphire and sardonyx |
| **WEDNESDAY** | • Wednesday is associated with Mercury, including the qualities of communication, intellect, wit, logic, intelligence, expression, technology, transportation, memory, curiosity and messages from spirits.<br>• *Crystals for Wednesday:* Amazonite, amber, aquamarine, blue lace agate, lapis lazuli, sapphire and sodalite |

**THURSDAY**

- Thursday is associated with Jupiter, including the qualities of luck, expansion, abundance, philosophy, higher learning, spiritual ideals, adventure, travel, cultural pursuits, boldness, courage, sovereignty, fortune and higher truth.
- *Crystals for Thursday*: Amber, amethyst, aventurine, carnelian, citrine, peacock ore, sugilite, tiger's eye, topaz, turquoise, yellow sapphire

**FRIDAY**

- Friday is associated with Venus, including the qualities of female sexuality, beauty, fertility, pleasure, wealth, sensuality, romance, receptivity, intimacy, self-care, creative expression, eroticism, devotion, passion, desire, allure and friendship.
- *Crystals for Friday*: Carnelian, celestite, citrine, emerald, green aventurine, jade, moonstone, pearl, rhodonite, rose quartz, ruby, tree moss agate

**SATURDAY**

- Saturday is associated with Saturn, including the qualities of authority, discipline, structure, rules, regulations, oppressive regimes, positive enforcements, time, society, law, order, power positions, karma and time.
- *Crystals for Saturday*: Amethyst, black tourmaline, blue sapphire, garnet, haematite, jet, lolite, obsidian, onyx, red jasper, shungite, smoky quartz

# Your Personal Spirit Team!

## Angels and ancestors

In addition to the archangels, there are other angels and energies working alongside your ancestors and spirit guides to help you.

### Elemental energies

You can work with the elemental energies to unlock hidden codes and ancient knowledge. For instance, each of the elements activates buried wisdom, as well as self-knowledge and memories linked to past, present and future lives.

- *Fire*: The Fire element is active, masculine, positive, light and dominant. Tools for healing with Fire include the sun, candles and the sacral and solar plexus chakras. Fire energy assists us with issues to do with energy, vitality, passion and ambition, as well as overcoming sexual and self-empowerment blocks. It can increase confidence, self-esteem and ambition, as well as optimism, excitement, adventure, fun and creative life-force. It is stimulating, electric and expressive.
- *Earth*: The Earth element is passive, feminine, negative, dark and receptive. Tools for healing with Earth include gemstones, crystals, plants, herbs,

trees and the root and heart chakras (grounding, touching and meditation exercises). Earth energy connects us to ancient wisdom, grounding, trustworthiness, dependability, practical awareness and our instincts. It can enhance responsibility, self-worth and resourcefulness.

- *Air*: The Air element is active, dominant, electric, expressive and cerebral. It's linked to communication, the intellect, logic, the imagination and intuition. Its energy is balancing, energizing and cooling, while sparking analytical and higher cerebral abilities, deep thought and potent observation and problem-solving. Tools for healing with Air include feathers, smudging (sage), incense and resins or palo santo, as well as the throat and third eye chakras.

- *Water*: The Water element is passive, magnetic, receptive, emotional and intuitive. It's linked to the qualities of femininity, empathy, nurturing, the imagination, creative genius, sensitivity, psychic gifts and spiritual powers. Tools for healing with Water include water of any kind and crystals that spark the sacral, third eye and crown chakras. Water energy can increase intuition, inspiration, divine revelations, emotional intelligence and the ability to feel, as well as romance, vulnerability and depth.

- *Ether/Spirit:* Ether or Spirit is also an element, and this is linked to the crown chakra. It amplifies faith, inspiration, spirituality, cosmic consciousness, universal love, compassion, divinity, hope, purity and self-realization. Tools for healing with Ether include transcendental meditation, fasting and crystals for the crown chakra. (Amethyst, clear quartz and selenite are my personal favourites.)

## Meditations for contacting and connecting

Meditation can be used to connect with any archangels or angels, also your guides or ancestors, and other beings as well. The only word of advice here is to genuinely know what each stands for, so you can develop a real, authentic connection with them – one that resonates with your heart!

# Connection meditation

First, create a sacred space. This can involve using incense, resin, palo santo, sage or other cleansing and clearing herbs or plants to clear your space. Tibetan singing bowls, bells and chimes, or binaural beats are great options too. Become present and mindful of your body and surroundings, and create a comfortable space within and around yourself.

Next, close your eyes and engage in some conscious breathing. You'll want to feel peaceful and calm in order to truly feel the effects of the meditation. You should be able to feel your heart beating softly if you're already in a serene or calm space, or powerfully if there are things you know you need to let go of. In your mind, just ask the angels or your spirit guides for healing and release. You may feel a warm glow in your heart.

The first stage is to synchronize your breathing with your heart as best you can. Spiritual beings enter our energy field and communicate with us through the heart chakra. This is where the archangels and angels work their magic, and where new insights arise. Without an active heart chakra, we can't receive guidance from spiritual beings or from our Higher Self.

Next, place your hands over your heart. Your hands are transmitters and receivers of life-force energy. This energy allows imbalances and blockages to be removed; it also helps increase energy flow and speed up self-healing, while leading to an expansion of consciousness. Everyone has the capacity to channel universal healing energy through their hands - it's a God-given gift.

Now your hands are in place and you are breathing at a steady and peaceful pace, picture something in your mind's eye that you wish to release. This may be a painful memory, a traumatic experience or a repressed or blocked emotion. It could be family trauma, loss or heartbreak... Angels and

archangels, as well as your spirit team, are able to
transmute any pain or traumatic memory you're holding on
to, taking it straight back through the Ether and spirit
realms to Source. All these beings act as channels to
transmute and take away what you request.

If you aren't trying to release anything, you can try the
opposite: asking your spirit team for what you want to
integrate or receive – a particular quality, strength or
blessing. Angels will also bestow what you need to thrive,
heal and attune to your best self.

Now hold that intention strong in your mind's eye.
See and feel it swirling through your heart. Assign a colour
to it – red if it involves pain, trauma or passion; orange if
it's related to emotions, friendships, romance, creativity or
intimacy; yellow if it's about self-empowerment, ambitions
or the ability to live with will-power and discipline; green if
it's related to the qualities of the heart; blue if it's about
self-expression, communication or clarity of thought and
perception; and violet or purple if it concerns greater
faith, intuition or cosmic awareness and universal
consciousness.

Envision a glowing light over and emanating from your
heart. This light can be gentle and any of the colours
outlined. As you see this beautiful and healing light
expanding, breathe into the memory or image of your
intention, filling it with the light. Or you can improvise and
see what your intuition tells you to do.

Visualize the light pouring into your heart, hands and the top of your head. Remember that meditation is about clearing as well as activating; you must create space within before you can recharge yourself.

Now set the intention to receive divine assistance. Call in one of the archangels, or someone from your spirit team, like a personal ancestor, guide or animal you know is supportive of you. Let them know of your intention and ask them for assistance, either with releasing or with embodying and integrating. Picture them clearly in your mind's eye, see an image of their true being... Reflect for a few minutes on their healing powers and the energy they can bring into your life.

Then, activate your intuition. Your intuition, as you now know, is connected to your Higher Self and is essential for angelic contact, spirit communication and receiving information, messages and wisdom from the Ether.

Sit for a while, alternating between feeling and thinking about or visualizing the various aspects of this meditation:

- Your intention
- The spiritual guide, ancestor, animal or angel you wish to connect with
- Their healing qualities and powers

Let the feeling of love and being protected in a warm and supportive embrace wash over you. Be open to receiving the healing light and rays of the spiritual realm.

Sit in this space, with your intuition activated, for as long as feels comfortable. If you feel any fear or doubt coming over you, breathe through it. Tension is the body's way of saying, 'I am healing! The divine light is working its magic...'

You can expand this meditation with the following. This is an extra component to amplify your psychic and intuitive gifts. Visualizing your future self is one of the fastest ways to align yourself with your ultimate self, your best life and your true north.

## Visualizing your future self

From the space you have created, picture your future self. Hold this image in your mind's eye, filling it with light. Envision yourself in an ethereal bubble of golden or white light; see it spilling into your auric field, radiating purity and divine healing light.

Be conscious of the auric field of your future self. It is here that you can receive messages, insights and divine or angelic wisdom. Your aura transmits messages from the Ether, the subconscious and the astral and soul planes and worlds. It connects you to an infinite source of wisdom and power, if you are open to receiving it.

So, picture yourself wrapped up in this golden embrace. Know that you are cherished, protected and supported. You have so much love and light to share.

Envision your life path and purpose, your soul's mission or your ideal life. Set an intention for your legacy to be made known.

Be mindful of the energy swirling around you in the present. Perhaps there are toxic traits and cycles you need to let go of. Perhaps you're holding on to things that don't serve you or your Higher Self. We tend to accumulate stories, false belief systems and faulty identities through the judgements of others. We pick up a lot that we cling on to, though really they don't serve us at all.

With the help of the angels and your spirit team, you can release all of these now. This is how you create space for fresh perspectives, wisdom and spiritual guidance. Your soul's plan trickles through to you when you heal and let go.

To end the meditation, bring your hands down gently to your knees. Sit still, with your palms relaxed and facing upwards or outwards. Relax and feel the energy flowing through, above and around them. Feel the peace within. You may begin to see lights or imagery, like astral visions! This is normal for those who are psychically inclined.

One final technique to stabilize this meditation is to incorporate some mantras or affirmations. You can get creative and come up with your own. Or you can try these:

☐ *'I open myself up to the divine light within. I accept the unconditional love and help of my angels and ancestors.'*

251

☐ 'I am receptive to all that God, the Great Spirit and the universe have to offer.'

☐ 'I fill myself with positive intentions, while making it clear that I wish to heal. I commit to cleansing and releasing my traumas and karma.'

Always remember that you are an empty vessel waiting to be filled. What are you filling yourself with?

## Crystal meditation
Meditation and harnessing the power of crystals work well together. Here are three crystal meditations for you:

# Universal flow

Start by placing your chosen crystal on your left hand with your palm face up but flat. Place your right hand over the top, an inch or so away. This meditation is all about giving and receiving energy, so remember your left hand is your receiving hand and your right hand is the giving hand. Placing the crystal on your left palm will therefore allow you to receive its healing energies while simultaneously giving (with your right). This amplifies your own natural healing power.

Take a few deep breaths and close your eyes. Set your intention, thanking the crystal in whichever way feels right for you with a short blessing.

Next, visualize a beautiful golden light being drawn in through your crown directly into the crystal. Take your time. With each breath, visualize and feel this loving, healing light energy radiating through your crown, charging the crystal. Due to the power of light energy from your crown chakra and the fact that your crystal will already be cleansed and charged, you should start to feel the effects pretty quickly!

You can stay in this energetic space and breathe golden light into your crystal for as long as you wish. Eventually, you may find you enter a transcendental state. Also, depending on the crystal or gemstone, you may begin to receive symbols, insights or direct wisdom from your Higher Self or angels.

When you feel the crystal is charged enough, you can either bask in the healing light and wisdom of the gemstone for a while, or place it on your altar or shrine. You may either keep it for future healing endeavours or receive its healing energy now.

The next meditation can be used to clear blocks from any of your chakras and charge them. To work on all seven of your main chakras, use clear quartz, otherwise choose a stone which resonates with you.

This meditation can be performed in just 5–10 minutes for a recharge or quick cleansing and balancing, or can become a longer crystal meditation.

You can sense which of your chakras needs work, if any, through pendulum dowsing. Set your intention and centre yourself. Then simply pass the pendulum over each of your chakras. The way it moves should inform you of which chakra(s) need clearing, balancing, healing, activating or aligning.

# Chakra charging

Begin by placing your crystal on your left hand with your palm face up but flat and place your right hand over the top, an inch or so away. Set your intentions, bless the crystal and charge it with the golden light visualization on page 252.

Now, breathe through and into your crown for about 10-12 breaths, then get in a meditative position and place your right hand underneath your left, creating a 'cup' with the crystal still on top.

Now bring your hands and the crystal up to the level of the chakra you wish to work on and begin to breathe into your hands. Visualize the coloured light energy of that particular chakra emanating from your hands into the crystal as you breathe: red for the root, orange for the sacral, yellow for the solar plexus, green for the heart, blue for the throat, purple for the third eye, white or violet for the crown.

With each breath, draw in this healing light energy, both seeing and feeling it swirl around the crystal and around your chakra. Synchronize your visualization so the light is around both.

Once you are in a synergistic flow and feel completely connected to the crystal and the chakra you are healing, project some intentions. The key is to set your intention, project it and then release it... The process of surrendering allows your chakra to fill up and the healing vibrations of the crystal to be amplified.

Once in the flow, you should begin to receive some visuals or images related to the energy of the chakra. You may even hear wisdom or guidance being spoken to you, through your clairaudient abilities. Subconscious guidance may shine through. Crystals open you up to the elemental world of subtle energy, thus there is infinite wisdom available to you, plus, of course, guidance from your spirit team. In short, your consciousness is activated.

The following meditation is fabulous for giving yourself a 'whole body awakening', and it's deeply blissful and euphoric and both relaxing and stimulating. It is especially powerful for releasing trapped energy in the body, for instance blocked emotions, repressed wounds, suppressed trauma, painful memories... It awakens your kundalini too, your primal and spiritual life-force, and helps with blocks to abundance, love and longevity. It's a miracle worker. Its effects are felt on the emotional, psychological, physical and spiritual planes, so although it releases blocks on an earthly level, it also connects you to a higher consciousness.

Moreover, it is helpful in removing psychic impurities, shielding you from psychic attack and protecting you. It aligns, balances and clears your chakras, while sparking soul growth. It connects you to your spirit team, instils deep peace and revitalizes your senses. Psychic and mediumship gifts are increased and amplified. And your auric field and ethereal body get a 'reboot' for further healing and transformation.

Ideally, your body should be purified for higher consciousness knowledge and insights to flow through you, so if you want to take this really seriously, you should engage in a one- or three-day fast or at least a juice or fruit cleanse and detox. This isn't essential, however.

Finally, you will need seven crystals relating to the seven main chakras and a further four quartz crystals, all cleansed, charged and programmed.

# Crystal grid meditation

Lie down comfortably in a space where you won't be disturbed and where there is no (or minimal) artificial lighting, just candles or natural light. Play soft background music and burn incense or any other Air tool (sage, resin, etc.) to clear the space.

Place the chakra crystals on the relevant chakras and one of the quartz crystals at the bottom of each foot, a few inches away. Another will be placed on your left palm once the meditation begins, and the last one goes about 6-7 inches above your crown chakra, completing an energetic 'crystal grid'.

Once you are lying down with your crystals in place, set your intentions and open yourself up to the healing energy. If you wish, you can say an affirmation, such as 'I am open to receiving the healing energy available' or 'My mind is open, my spirit is receptive and my heart is pure.' You can create your own if you prefer.

The quartz crystal on your left hand during the meditation is there to receive any energies that wish to come through, remembering that your left hand is known as the receiving hand. Keep your palm chakra open to receive, as this leads to shifts in vibration. Your frequency will elevate, which in turn will heal you on multiple levels.

You can place your hands over any of your chakras during the meditation, if that feels comfortable to you. Or you can keep them on key areas like your root, sacral, solar plexus, heart or third eye (these tend to be the easiest). Work intuitively. Trust what your body wants. Let it speak to you.

YOU MUST BE PSYCHIC

## Tree meditation

Crystals are great for meditation, and so are trees! Trees are ancient, mighty and strong. They have deep roots, through which they receive powerful healing energy which can help us achieve longevity and good health. Simultaneously, their crowns connect them to the Ether, spiritual world and soul planes.

# Tree meditation for grounding and connection

Find a quiet and comfortable place outside, where there is a tree which resonates with you, one you feel drawn to.

Sit down with your knees bent, feet flat on the earth and back straight against the trunk of the tree. Socks and shoes off! Your feet should be 'at one' with the earth. Did you know that your feet have chakras too? Now you do.

Gently rest against the trunk, starting to feel universal life-force energy flowing through you in unison with the tree.

Start with 10–12 conscious breaths and close your eyes, bringing your awareness inside yourself and then to the tree.

Once you feel centred, begin to visualize a loving but gentle golden light travelling up through your feet and up your spine to the top of your head. Breathe slowly and deeply. With each breath, visualize this loving light travelling through you.

Meditate on your similarity to the tree as you breathe: how your feet are linked to the earth; how your spine is like the trunk; and how your crown is similar to the crown of the tree, with its leaves serving as ethereal cords to the infinite, to the Great Unknown. This is actually what they are.

Repeat this beautiful synergy visualization as many times as you wish, starting at your feet/roots and ending with your crown/leaves connecting to the Ether. Then go the other way, from the crown to the roots. Go up and then go down.

Eventually, you will feel a spiralling motion and will begin to feel the tree's energy merging with your own. You will alternate between feeling your own energy and the tree's. In other words, you will feel the essence of you both separately and as two interconnected entities. This creates a divine experience. And it works! Trust me, it's an amazing sensation.

Once you are in a steady flow and experiencing blissful and euphoric or healing and calming sensations, imagine the golden light travelling up the tree.

Synchronize your breath with the tree's. After a while, you will start to feel your heartbeat and the tree's as one. You may even feel a strong swirl of energy on your back, as if the tree is communicating with you. Remember, we are all connected. You and the tree are one, so you can receive powerful messages from it, along with life-force and inspirational qualities that connect you to your innate spiritual gifts.

As you continue with the meditation, your soul awakens, your Higher Self sparks into life and you become more magnificent in your personal power and integrity.

To enhance this experience, bring a quartz or any other crystal with you.

# FINAL WORDS

As this book comes to a close, and you continue on with your journey, whatever, wherever and however that may be, I would like to extend my gratitude to you for joining me on this journey, for having faith and for trusting me to help and guide you.

It's so important within this spiritual world to take what resonates with you and leave what doesn't. I firmly believe in this. Whatever anyone shares with you, you should only take what truly resonates and let the rest go.

With that being said, everything I have shared with you throughout this book has not only come from the heart but also with the intention to bring you clarity, insight and direction on your spiritual journey.

I have complete faith in my abilities, and if this is the path you choose to follow, then I hope this has instilled some confidence in you, and clarified some of the areas that perhaps you have been unsure about.

I'd like to leave you with a few reminders and final thoughts that should help you continue to develop your spiritual gifts and embrace the natural intuition that we all have within us. That's actually a good place to start:

## We all have intuition

Intuition is something completely natural that is within each and every one of us. We are all born with it. We often receive intuitive feelings and thoughts in our day-to-day lives without even realizing, and often we dismiss them as coincidences or choose to ignore them due to a lack of trust. But trust your intuition. It is there. You do have it.

## Embrace your individuality

There is no rule-book for this journey we are on. Your spiritual journey may differ from that of someone else. You are an individual, your own person. Be free to walk away or distance yourself from anything that does not align or resonate with you.

## You are enough

You are enough and have always been enough. Everything that you need is already within you. To live a spiritual life, all you need is yourself ... and good intentions.

## Be loving and kind to yourself

It is so important to remember that we are human – we are humans having an earthly experience. This has been one of my most significant lessons on my spiritual journey thus far. We are human and it is OK to feel the way we feel, but we should be kinder, gentler and more loving towards ourselves, especially when we need love and kindness.

## Your psychic abilities, intuition and spiritual gifts are not to be hidden away

Be proud of who you are, go forward fearlessly and trust in yourself and the universe. May you feel the love and support of your spirit family and know that you are never alone.

I will leave you with a few affirmations to end your practice with...

'I am so psychic.'

'I easily sense the presence of my loved ones in spirit.'

'Every day my intuition grows stronger and stronger.'

'My guardian angels and spirit guides are blessing me now and always.'

'My spirit guides light up the path before me. They
   help me to see clearly.'

'I am enough.'

'I am safe.'

'I am protected.'

'I am loved.'